MW01140498

# 42 Rules for Effective Connections

### By Bonnie Ross-Parker and Cindy Elsberry

E-mail: info@superstarpress.com
20660 Stevens Creek Blvd., Suite 210
Cupertino, CA 95014

First Printing: August 2009
Paperback ISBN: 978-1-60773-046-0 (1-60773-046-4)
Place of Publication: Silicon Valley, California, USA
Library of Congress Number: 2009933220

eBook ISBN: 978-1-60773-047-7 (1-60773-047-2)

## Trademarks

All terms mentioned in this book that are known to be trademarks or service marks have been appropriately capitalized. Super Star Press™ cannot attest to the accuracy of this information. Use of a term in this book should not be regarded as affecting the validity of any trademark or service mark.

## Warning and Disclaimer

Every effort has been made to make this book as complete and as accurate as possible, but no warranty of fitness is implied. The information provided is on an "as is" basis. The authors, contributors, and publisher shall have neither liability nor responsibility to any person or entity with respect to any loss or damages arising from the information contained in the book.

If you do not wish to be bound by the above, you may return this book to the publisher for a full refund.

# Praise For This Book!

"Bonnie Ross-Parker inspires you to leave your imprint everywhere you go, by making every connection with everyone count. Learn to fall in love with the anticipation of meeting new people, and build lasting relationships with them. For anyone who wants to improve their communication skills, '42 Rules for Effective Connections' is the book for you."
**Debbie Madiou, President, Liveonlinemeeting.com**

"'42 Rules for Effective Connections' is not just an idle suggestion when coming from Bonnie Ross-Parker and Cindy Elsberry. After experiencing the passionate and authentic 'voice' of contributing writers you'll quickly see that what they provide are the *concise, practical* steps to truly experiencing the joy of connecting with others and getting better results TODAY!"
**Mary K Weinhagen, Editor,**
http://www.TheNetworkMarketingMagazine.com,
maryk@mkweinhagen.com

"I've often said it's who you know that gets you in the door, and what you know that keeps you there. '42 Rules for Effective Connections' is about both of these—building meaningful connections that open doors, and sharing yourself with integrity so that you sustain lasting relationships. It's a great book to read cover to cover or to just pick up when you have a moment or two. One idea could change your life."
**Marnie Pehrson, CEO/Founder,** http://www.ideamarketers.com

# Acknowledgements

As with any book, the support, encouragement, efforts and activity 'behind the scenes' are the elements that, together, make the final product a reality. I am especially grateful to those amazing licensees of The Joy of Connecting® who stepped up to share their ideas and expertise so that readers everywhere could benefit from their experiences. I also want to thank the friends of our community who decided to share their thoughts on how we can all connect more effectively. Hats off to our entire team of 42 writers.

For a long time, it was my dream to have a book that reflected the greatness of The Joy of Connecting® community, and now that vision has manifested! When our request went out for potential participating contributors, Cindy and I were inspired by the fresh ideas, the diversity of strategies and the expertise that showed up. I doubt that on our own we could've ever reached the excellence that combined efforts produced.

My co-editor, Cindy Elsberry, masterfully put this entire project together. She did all the collecting, editing, re-editing and arranging. I believe the final product speaks to her selfless commitment to make '42 Rules for Effective Connections' a first class book. No words of appreciation could adequately describe my gratitude to her. As my virtual assistant and friend, I value Cindy's spirit, loyalty and expertise. Because of you, Cindy, this book will have lasting value for years to come. Thank you for being my partner in this wonderful project.

Bonnie Ross-Parker
CEO/Founder of The Joy of Connecting®

# Contents

Contents

# Foreword

We all recognize the value and importance of relationships in both our personal and professional lives. Often, it's helpful to 'step back' to consider whether we could be more effective, communicate to achieve greater results and leave a positive, memorable impact in the way we present ourselves.

When I read Bonnie and Cindy's collaborative book, '42 Rules for Effective Connections,' I thought that finally we have an innovative, stand out, easy to read resource to improve and enhance not only our casual encounters, but the ones we are looking to strengthen in the business community as well!

Their book is filled with fresh ideas, easy to implement strategies and a wealth of personal experiences. You can start anywhere. Read any rule and by the time you've digested all 42, you can't help but become a connections expert. All it takes is a little time and willingness to implement what you have learned.

I encourage you to take '42 Rules for Effective Connections' seriously if you want to improve the quality of your connections. After all, the marketplace is crowded. Everyone is vying for their share of attention and dollars. You now have in your hands a small, powerful resource serving as a guidebook to better connections for better results. Enjoy the journey!

**Nicki Keohohou**
**CEO/Co-Founder**
**DSWA/The Direct Selling Women's Alliance**

*Tired of the same ole networking chatter? Do you think anyone is really listening to what you have to say? Wish you were somewhere else? Do you believe there is a better way to expand business than standing at a bar with a drink in one hand and a plate of warmed over chicken wings in the other?* If you have to network to grow your business and find yourself spending money going to events, meeting as many people as possible and returning to the office with a handful of business cards without the results you want, you can benefit from the strategies presented in '42 Rules for Effective Connections.'

With significant combined years of networking experience behind this project, we decided to collaborate with great connectors to bring you proven, applicable ideas to strengthen your ability to dialogue with anyone at anytime to achieve the best outcome possible. Each of our contributing writers was asked, *What do you think makes you an effective connector and what do you think others would say about you?* Their answers are the basis of this book. Women wrote stories around what they are passionate about when it comes to being an effective connector. They wrote from their heart and experiences.

As co-editors, we were surprised and inspired by the ideas/strategies that women shared. Had we been doing this on our own, there is no question that we would have fallen short in identifying the diversity of responses we uncovered. This book runs through a complete and enlightening range of ideas.

For anyone who wants to improve communication, get better results in any networking environment and alleviate the stress and anxiety that comes from building a business where you have to go out to meet potential customers '42 Rules for Effective Connections' is a must-read. The contributing writers provide a broad range of strategies that make the difference between networking that is 'hit or miss'—'trial and error' versus networking that hits the bull's eye. If you are serious about growing your business and simply are missing the mark on how to make your behavior stand out or if you are achieving success already and want to step up your game, this book will open the door to new possibilities.

There are literally thousands of networking events available for anyone wanting to attend. All you do is go online and search for associations and organizations in your area. They welcome your participation and your membership. You can continue to show up as you have in the past and get the same results you'd anticipate. If your results are exactly what you're looking for, that's terrific. Maybe, however, the investment of both your time and dollars is not producing the business you want! '42 Rules for Effective Connections' is not about which meeting to attend; it is about how to get better results when you arrive! In this book you will learn:

- How to position yourself in a crowded market-place.
- How to start conversations.
- What to say to make yourself memorable.
- How to ensure that others will want to do business with you.
- How to improve your performance and the outcome.

It is our hope that the benefit you receive from reading '42 Rules for Effective Connections' will equal the joy we experienced in bringing this book to you.

**Bonnie Ross-Parker and Cindy Elsberry
Co-Editors**

# 1

# Rules Are Meant To Be Broken

**Cindy Elsberry and Bonnie Ross-Parker**

*We have the freedom to create our own rules as long as they don't cause others harm.*

Since the dawn of civilization, we have created ways to communicate and connect with each other for various reasons. Without communication, humans could not function in a successful, progressive society. We communicate with more than words, whether in spoken or written form. Our facial expressions, body language, attire and even our choice of jewelry can convey non-verbal messages to those around us. How others perceive those messages is the first step in communication. Without communication we make no connections. Whether your purpose is business related or not, every connection you make has the chance to propel you toward enhancing your life in general. Everyone is a unique individual; we have our own ways of connecting with other people. One person may prefer face-to-face contact and handwritten notes; another may prefer social networking online and emails as a way to connect with others.

Have you noticed how rules change over time? Not long ago, corporate America, known for a strict coat and tie dress code, decided one day to implement 'Casual Friday.' Remember our moms telling us that every gift deserved a hand-written 'thank you' note? While still a practice deserving continuation, we know that a quick phone call or email seems more widely accepted. How about the rule that you must wait at least 20 minutes after eating before going swimming? Fact or fiction?

Who makes the rules anyway? Sure, we need to enforce policies designed to protect us, ensure equality and keep society from chaos. We do, however, have the freedom to create our own rules as long as they don't cause others harm. Kids dress in ways today that would never have been acceptable years ago; lifestyles adjust according to individual choice. We have come to accept change because change occurs with or without our acceptance.

We are on the journey called 'life' together. We believe each of us possesses the ability to connect with one another more effectively. While there are no right or wrong rules when it comes to connecting, with the right strategies you have the ability to live a fuller, more successful and more joyous life. It's simple. Choose appropriate and positive behavior to connect in ways that foster relationships, honor individuality and bring you the results you want.

'42 Rules for Effective Connections' was created as an innovative guide for those that wish to make more successful and satisfying connections in their professional and personal lives. The rules were contributed by women who have offered not only traditional ways to make effective connections but ways to step outside the box as well. They provide ideas and strategies that, when implemented, left a positive imprint on others, and decided to generously share these ideas with you.

Although every individual must connect with other individuals, that connection can be made in a variety of ways. Every rule outlined in this book may or may not apply to your personal style or preference. However, finding the rules that you can bend or break in order to implement more successful connections is the goal of this publication.

# 2 Make Every Connection Count

**Bonnie Ross-Parker**

**Uncovering special people is a skill worth developing. Special people exist everywhere.**

I've been and continue to be a networking 'junkie.' Networking is in my blood right along with oxygen. I'm addicted! I love the anticipation of meeting new people and uncovering new talent and the satisfaction of introducing people to others they need to meet! For me, networking is like a walk on the beach—you simply never know the outcome of any encounter—no different from finding one special shell that stands out from the rest because of its size, its beauty or uniqueness. You pick it up, hold it in your hand and take it with you. Uncovering special people is a skill worth developing. Special people exist everywhere.

What I've frequently discovered during networking experiences, however, is how quickly someone can dismiss another person because they don't look beyond the surface of the individual to what is unseen. How can anyone know the talent one has, the resource someone can offer, the opportunity that a connection can generate if a quick glance is all that is offered? Only through a conversation, an exchange of ideas and a door open to possibilities can anyone really know the value one individual can offer to the life of another. That's why I adhere to the mantra: *Make Every Connection Count!*

There's no magic and no special skills or strategy to make this happen. You simply treat everyone you meet with a smile, with acknowledgement and respect. You express appreciation to the clerk who tenders your order at the supermarket, the teller who handles your bank transaction, the postal employee who delivers your mail, the clerk who hands you your clean laundry and anyone else who serves or impacts you in some way. Replace 'Thank you' with 'I appreciate you.' Get in the habit of expressing this anytime you can under any circumstance and you will soon discover that making every connection count becomes natural and joyful. Someone holds the door open for you? "I appreciate you did that for me!" Someone does you a favor? Express appreciation. Make acknowledgement a habit.

Once I got in the swing of going the extra mile to bring value to even casual connections, I stepped up my game in the networking arena. I don't let any opportunity pass me by to make connections count. Others will say, "Make a good impression." I translate that to "Leave indelible positive imprints everywhere you go and in everything you do." You never know where a positive connection can lead. You never know the difference you can make in someone's life or the difference someone can make in yours. *You never know!*

I once had a casual conversation with a young woman I met at a Chamber of Commerce 'after hours' that ultimately led to a speaking engagement in Germany! Not long ago, I met a business coach at a networking event and introduced him to an amazing woman who was developing an innovative training program. They became partners! You might be thinking, "Will I ever get rewarded for having a generous spirit?" My answer is "Yes." The rule is simple. *Make every connection count.* Let others sing your praises and be raving fans. Do what you do out of integrity and you will experience rewards for your efforts. Sometimes, acknowledgement comes from an unexpected source, a circumstance you've long forgotten or because you gave someone your full attention. Just know that by making every connection count you are paving the way for incredible results.

# You Are The Key

**Cindy Borassi**

Imagine you're sitting at a Chamber of Commerce breakfast with 300 of your closest business acquaintances and it's your turn to do your 30-second elevator speech. What would you say in one sentence to convey what you do? Offer? Have to give? What is your unique gift to the world? And, why would they stop chewing their pancakes or fruit salad to listen to you? No answer, that's okay. Chances are 95% of those 300 attendees do not know the answer to these questions either.

The key to successful connections is in knowing where to begin. With *you!* What is the one thing you do really well? What is your unique gift? What is your purpose in life? Who do you want to become?

When you have the answers and know who you are and who you want to become you can be of service to that truth every time you connect with someone. Once you make the commitment to get clear on your purpose and to let your purpose manifest in your life, the universe will start providing you with endless opportunities and effortless connections.

If you are clear on your vision for yourself and are willing to take action and live into your purpose, you will begin to attract like-minded people to you. This is where discrimination comes into play. Once you get clear the universe will bombard you with clues and opportunities. Pay attention to each connection you make during the day…they are all providing you with clues and opportunities. Step into each connection with the intention of being of service to your truth and where you want to be and the connection becomes an opportunity to share your unique gift, vision and message.

Once you've laid the groundwork you will find that the connections presented to you are there for a very specific reason—they have a unique gift that supports your purpose in life as well.

Are you ready? Good—stop making excuses and make your preparations for stepping into something big in your life. *You!*

## How to Get Clear On YOU

* Spend time each day reflecting on your unique gifts and talents.
* Become aware of that light within you which is your special purpose in life.
* Be specific about who you are and who you want to become.
* Share these discoveries with your support network, friends, and family—those who will boost your confidence.
* Reflect on whether you are truly ready for something big in your life, abundance and prosperity.
* Release negative emotional blocks to receiving the gifts the universe supplies to help you become who you want to be.
* Develop your message—personal and professional.
* Tune into your subconscious mind and your self-talk—saturate it with your purpose, a grand vision for yourself and your life.
* Notice what, and more importantly who, shows up in your life!
* Be grateful.

# 4 Honor Your Commitments

### R. Jill Fink

**It's possible to keep your commitments, build your credibility, and garner the respect of your peers, all while making sure your stress levels are low and productivity is high.**

When we make commitments to others, we tend to keep them. However, life happens, and we sometimes get off track. We lose our focus, which could lead to losing a sale or an important connection. Even worse, we lose our credibility and the respect of those we have let down...and we lose respect for ourselves. Another 'side effect' of not honoring our commitments is we cause ourselves undue stress.

What keeps us from honoring commitments we have made to others and/or to ourselves? Two important things can stand in our way: Undeveloped skills in decision-making and poor planning. When you commit to something, you are making a pledge. Was this pledge a good idea? How are you going to see it through to the end? What is the downside to not meeting your commitment? How do you go about raising your probability of success?

Not to worry: It's possible to keep your commitments, build your credibility, and garner the respect of your peers, all while making sure your stress levels are low and productivity is high. How can you do all of that without finding twenty-four more hours in each day? By utilizing the seven secrets below:

**Keep it simple.** Take it one week, one day, or even one hour at a time. Don't make huge promises that you cannot keep. Managing your time (and stress level) in simple terms can increase your success rate instead of setting you up for failure.

**Keep it realistic.** Can you *really* make that deadline, or will it take you another day or two? What is the reality that you can truly commit?

**Plan ahead.** Literally! Get a planner, whether it's digital or in print, and utilize it to its maximum potential. Check it, revise it, read it and use it every day. Write down what you need, want and wish you could do. This ties in with secret #1, and will allow you to bite off only that which you can easily chew.

**Take action.** You've promised and you've planned. The date has arrived. Now, do it! Honor yourself and the other person by making it on time. Show up prepared and with a smile.

**Follow through.** You met your commitment, but you're not finished! Follow-up is a good way to keep the connection alive. Tell people when they can next expect to hear from you. (Then write a "note to self" in your planner to contact them.) Send a hand-written note of thanks. Check in with them periodically just to see how they are doing.

**Say what you mean, and mean what you say.** People prefer to do business with people they know, like, and trust. If you say you will do it, then do it. If you mean to be of assistance, tell them so. But don't say things you don't mean or make promises you know you won't keep.

**Create a positive and supportive environment for yourself.** High self-esteem is a key factor in keeping a positive attitude and attracting positive people to your life. In turn, self-doubt is diminished and your network of friends and contacts can support you in any time of need, whether it's as simple as picking up dry cleaning or as complex as helping you prepare a major presentation to potential clients. Hold brainstorming sessions. Take time for yourself and your family. Tell yourself that you can. Meeting your commitments and your goals will naturally fall into place.

When you honor commitments and keep your promises it sets a good example for your family, friends and business associates. Every one of them will know they can count on you, and in turn, will be more likely to keep their promises to you and to anyone else they meet. It's a positive practice that can only yield positive results.

# Be Persistent, Not a Pest

**Valerie Pierce**

**Persistence is trial and error and usually requires many attempts before any progress is seen.**

From the Merriam Webster online dictionary:

Persistent -

1) existing for a long or longer than usual time or continuously as: a) retained beyond the usual period b) continuing without change in function or structure

2) a) continuing or inclined to persist in a course b) continuing to exist despite interference or treatment

My family has always said I didn't have a first word but rather an entire paragraph. At an early age, I learned that really connecting required persistence.

In my various businesses, I studied the best ways to form relationships. As a result of my studies, I adopted a lifetime rule of persistence. I asked questions and became involved through active dialogue. The area where my tanning salon was located was extremely expensive to advertise. So, I used the rule of persistence by facilitating heavy grass roots marketing concepts. I marketed heavily to the community by direct mail, phone calls, and business to business. As a result, among many other wonderful opportunities, a popular radio station gave my salon free airtime and event promotion.

As a child, I learned to perfect the skill of persistence in building relationships. I was in 2nd grade and everyone in my church was to give up one thing for several weeks. On my own, I chose television. It was difficult because the other kids were still watching TV and I had nothing to discuss. And still, I stayed on course.

As an adult, persistence has developed into a crucial tool for success. I use this tool to build my business. The old saying goes something like: People don't care how much you know until they know how much you care. With my cosmetics business, I had set a goal of talking to 1,000 people. I set that goal and went for it person after person after person. My goal was not 'milk money' out of the 1,000, but rather to extend my network base and to gain more experience. At one point, my supervisor called me and said, "Do you realize that if you worked just a little harder, you could make #1 in sales for our unit?" I chose to alter my goal by using my skill of being persistent to follow up with my contacts. I came 'close but no cigar' to my goal of meeting 1,000 people. However, I ended up talking to 641 people! Because of that I earned the #1 position for sales in my unit and was crowned 'Queen of Sales.'

Making an effective connection requires adopting the rule of persistence. Persistence is trial and error and usually requires many attempts before any progress is seen. Leaving nothing to chance, you make the first move and the subsequent moves after. It is not a pride issue; it is a perseverance issue. Sometimes it takes a lifetime to cultivate the skill.

# 6 Take a Chance—Put Yourself Out There

Antoinette Corbin

**My dream meant absolutely nothing as long as I held on to it and let it be just a dream. I had to give others a chance to get to know me, share my dreams and visions, and go from there.**

I have dreamed of becoming a successful author since my junior year in high school, when we were given a creative writing assignment to complete in English class. English was (and is) my favorite subject, so this new assignment was an exciting challenge. I scored well on the paper, and thus my love of and for writing was born, along with my dream.

Now, the only drawback to my lofty ambitions is that I'm a bit of a wallflower. I'm very shy and not at all outgoing. Born to a shy, quiet, 22-year-old single mom, and teased mercilessly in elementary school, the last thing I ever wanted to do at any time was approach people. The very thought terrified me. I was never one for the limelight or center stage; I made sure all my high school extracurricular activities were ones in which I could blend into the background (band for example). Eventually, in college, I ventured out, joining the Drama Club and playing lead in the year-end production. I even wrote a few articles for the university newspaper. Still, I silently held onto my dream.

I have previously done some publicized writing. Some years ago I wrote a poem for a going-away party for a supervisor at a local department store where I worked. One of my co-workers liked it so much she asked me to do a poem for her mother's birthday celebration. The family enjoyed it tremendously, and she asked me to do it again year after year for a few years. I was delighted when she asked me to do a special poem for her daughter's wedding. That was a real high point for me.

Still, I felt I needed more of an outlet for my writings, my ideas and opinions. I held onto and nursed my dream for quite a while, until a few months ago. While browsing online, I discovered a site geared toward writers. I took a chance and joined, and found it to be a very pleasant experience. Eventually, I started being recruited for other similar sites as well as sites geared toward women entrepreneurs and stay-at-home moms. I found a wonderfully amazing camaraderie from other women who had similar ambitions, and who gave me their unconditional support and encouragement. Ultimately, I began posting blogs and poetry I'd written, and the response was awesome. One of my poems even won the prize in a contest on one of the sites. I was so excited! I had finally found the starting gate for my dream.

So what am I saying? I'm saying, had I not just taken the chance and joined those sites, I would not be on the path I am now, experiencing this opportunity. I had to take a chance, take a step, and put myself out there. My dream meant absolutely nothing as long as I held on to it and let it be just a dream. I had to give others a chance to get to know me, share my dreams and visions, and go from there. I have received amazingly positive feedback on the work I have posted, and made some wonderful friends in the process. I've met people who are already published, and they've been only too happy to share tips and information on getting published. Taking a chance and putting myself out there is how I ended up connected with The 5-Second Commute, and thus ended up here.

Do you have a dream that you're nursing? Are you longing to share your vision and your passion with others, and enjoy a successful career through that passion at the same time? Then go ahead: Take A Chance, Take A Step, and Put Yourself Out There. Like me, you will be so glad you did.

# 7 Keep a Curious Mind

**Susan Brown**

**Curiosity is a vital, risk-free networking tool.**

I grant you that being curious can have dangerous side effects. You have probably heard the phrase 'curiosity killed the cat' and read about the exploits of Curious George, the famous monkey whose extreme inquisitiveness spawned mayhem and mishap. However, I assure you that curiosity is a vital, risk-free networking tool.

I love trying to discover people's hidden passions. I once asked a woman at a Joy of Connecting meeting what she loved to do but was not doing. When she said 'teaching' I knew I had found a co-facilitator for one of my workshops for not only was she an expert in her field but she had a passion waiting to be tapped. That single response yielded a great return on my investment of one curious question.

I am also really curious about people's values. At a networking luncheon I found myself next to a woman who had just reached the upper echelons of Mary Kay Cosmetics and had the coveted pink car to prove it. I have to admit that I initially thought that we would have very little to talk about as our companies, coaching and cosmetics, seemed worlds apart. But then, thankfully, my curiosity about her success kicked in: "What do you do that makes you so successful?"

She perked up and told me that her success was due to her persistence, passion and practice. Those memorable answers came straight from her heart revealing her values. By finding out what really 'drives' her success, I was rewarded with a deeper connection, a great success story and several success qualities to integrate into my Boot Camps for Success.

**Cu-ri-ous** (*Adjective*): Eager to learn or know; inquisitive.

The nosy neighbor who may be shunned for being too 'eager to learn or know' would be welcome for this 'virtuous' trait at a networking event. Elias Baumgarten in 'Curiosity as a Moral Virtue' says:

*Curiosity is especially important in deepening one's care and concern for another person because even in a close relationship, much that one needs to know and understand about another person in order to care deeply will not be apparent without active seeking.*[1]

How can you use your curiosity to develop more interesting and deeper relationships? It's perfectly fine to start with the usual kinds of questions we all ask:

* What do you do?
* How long have you been in business?
* How did you get started?
* Who are your clients?

After one or two of these questions, shift into the land of curiosity where the treasures are hiding. I have found it much easier to connect with and care for people when they answer questions about their values, dreams, desires, passions or challenges:

* What has been your greatest job challenge? How did you overcome it?
* What do you like best about what you do?
* To what do you attribute your success?
* What do you do in your job that gives you the most energy?
* What are you hoping to get out of this event (networking, conference, class)?

Don't be afraid to show you care by asking curious, thoughtful questions that stimulate meaningful conversations. You will be rewarded by responses that are like puzzle pieces waiting to be connected to reveal more of the real, whole person.

If you are willing to go confidently into uncharted territory with a detective mindset and a caring attitude, you will enhance your connections. I guarantee that by exercising a curious mind not only will you survive (unlike the poor cat) but also your relationships will thrive.

---

1. Excerpt from the essay published in the 'International Journal of Applied Philosophy,' Fall 2001

# 8 Be Transparent

C. Denese Sampson

**Take joy in knowing that your willingness to be transparent made a lasting connection that will affect another's life.**

In making connections, I have learned not to be afraid of exposing the flaws and mistakes I've made along the way. I have learned that the more I lean on the side of transparency regarding who I am and where I stand, the connections I make are much more meaningful and lasting. Transparency is a powerful tool that links you to your audience, whoever that may be, and creates an unbelievable bond. Learn to maximize your connections through the power of transparency.

Although I've always considered myself a 'people person,' the idea of connecting with people through social networking is very new to me, and it has taken some adjustment to find my comfort zone. I have had to get used to the idea of promoting myself and my company without feeling like I'm overwhelming my listener with tedious details they really could do without. But to be more effective in your connections, and to make connections that really last, learning how to open up about your fears and your worries, your trials as well as your triumphs, will lend a sense of authenticity that has a lasting positive effect on you and your audience.

I first realized the power of transparency at a Women's Conference with my church. We had gone through a day of customized events and plenary seminars, and were settling around a cozy fire to share funny stories and testimonies. As the night progressed one of my dearest friends, a young lady much younger than me whose friendship I value, told me I inspired her. She said my willingness to be transparent about the difficulties and joys of marriage, childrearing, and just life in general, encouraged her to push for a higher mark in her own life. Until that day, I never knew how meaningful one's transparency can be to someone else's life. I never really considered how important it is to allow the open and candid sharing of my life's journey to serve as inspiration for another's journey.

The power of transparency can help others overcome seemingly insurmountable adversity. Transparency can inspire someone who either shares your concerns or has experienced similar woes to keep moving forward. The power of your transparency can be transformed into the stimulus that catapults the object of your connection to the next level, ultimately leading to victory over adversity.

You may never know how your willingness to be transparent helps someone in their own struggles. Some people are not able to be so candid in sharing, and that's okay. But on that day when someone walks up to you and says, *Thank you so much for sharing your story—I thought I was alone, but you've helped me and inspired me to move on*, you can take joy in the fact that your struggle, and that of many people like you, was not in vain. Take joy in knowing that your willingness to be transparent made a lasting connection that will affect another's life in the most positive way, bringing personal triumph and satisfaction one step closer.

# 9

# Learn To Listen

**Cindy Elsberry**

**Many people have poor listening skills; luckily it is a skill which anyone can improve.**

"Are you listening to me?" is a question we've all been asked by a relative, friend, or business associate. Being heard makes us feel validated and understood. However, many people have poor listening skills. Luckily, it is a skill which anyone can improve.

One of the skills of a good listener is having a clear mind while listening to someone. The time to worry about your problems should come later, when you are not having a conversation. You need to focus 100% of your attention on the speaker. What if you miss important information?

Another skill to develop is not interrupting. Hold your opinion, idea or advice until they either ask a question or take a sufficient pause that would welcome a comment. By truly paying attention, you show respect for what they are saying, conveying the message that what is important to them is important to you as well.

Ever since I was a teenager I have been known to be a good listener. Friends and family have come to me countless times because they've needed an ear to bend. Because I listened, I became the 'go to' person. This talent has carried over into my professional life as well. Listening helps me build close, successful relationships with my clients.

Active listening is vital in building rapport, especially in any new relationship. For example, at networking events, it is good practice to not only listen when the speaker is giving their 'elevator speech,' but before and after the meetings when everyone engages in more personal conversations. Recently, a potential client called me. It had been about a month since I had last seen her. She stated her name and asked if I remembered who she was. I said, "Of course I remember you." I then proceeded to recall some of our previous conversation. At that time, she had made a few casual comments about how rushed her day had been and how tired she was. When I recalled those simple details, she paused for a moment and said, "Wow, you are *good*." Demonstrating to her that I'd been listening made her feel special.

As you are listening, eye contact is very important. When your mind wanders, your eyes glaze over and the faraway look on your face reveals to the speaker that you aren't paying attention. At a networking event, a woman was talking to the group. I maintained eye contact with her throughout her presentation. I noticed that she kept looking in my direction while she was speaking. A few weeks later, she called to hire me for a project. As we were talking, she mentioned that night at the networking meeting and said that she could tell that I really 'got her.' Had I not been listening and making eye contact, I would have lost out on an important connection.

When you establish eye contact with your speaker, try to be aware of the non-verbal signals you are sending in response to what the speaker is saying. Nodding, facing the person directly instead of indirectly, and smiling at appropriate times are all examples of non-verbal communication that lets the speaker know they are being heard. If you must look away, looking down at the floor for a second or two keeps your eyes from wandering about the room and gives the speaker the impression that you are giving thought to their message.

Building your listening skills may be a lot easier than you think. The next time you are involved in a conversation, try to incorporate the aforementioned attributes of being a good listener. If you find yourself getting distracted, try repeating back some of the key points of the conversation. Don't be afraid to ask questions if you are not clear on what the speaker is saying. With a little practice, listening will become second nature.

# Genuinely Care For Others

**Marcie Hooks**

**It is easy to form relationships when you genuinely care.**

I was one of nine children born and reared in the southern United States. My parents were loving, honest, caring and hard working. We were taught true southern hospitality, to 'care for our neighbor,' not be selfish and to love our brothers and sisters (even when we did not want to). We learned by example.

My mother was extremely wise, gentle and very soft-spoken. In fact, during her lifetime she never raised her voice to any of us no matter what mischief we were up to. (We really believed that she had eyes in the back of her head and kept them covered with hair just so we couldn't see her looking at us.) Lying was not tolerated nor was the mistreatment of any human being. We learned to genuinely care for one another, tell the truth and be sincere. We applied those teachings and carried them with us into our adult life.

The saying, "People do not care how much you know until they know how much you care" has stayed with me. The results of that teaching have helped me to be warm and sincere with people I am around, and I attribute my success to my parents for that teaching since I have been successful with both my chosen careers.

Warmth and sincerity is such a part of me that I do not think about it—I just project it and I am so thankful for those qualities. The results are that I have met a lot of acquaintances and friends of many years. It is easy to form connections when you genuinely care. There are many people who are looking for someone who genuinely cares for them. When someone is standing off by themselves, or acting shy, it is hard to tell if they want to be by themselves or have had a bad day or if they are longing for someone to talk to; someone to show a little interest or just wishing someone would speak to them.

It doesn't take a genius to tell if one is sincere or just pretending to be. I am successful because I sincerely want to help people. I keep the person's best interest in front of me. Our connection helps me show them the best way to make money and to strategize a successful future for them.

# Invest In Yourself

**Vicki Wallace**

**We have entered the information age, and education is more important than ever!**

I have always believed and been passionate about connecting and building relationships. I have been blessed to work in multiple roles where I have interacted with many incredibly talented women and men. I was in corporate America working for a Fortune 500 company for 20+ years, was the National Executive Director for a women's networking association for many years and have had the opportunity to work side-by-side with experts such as Brian Tracy, Mark Victor Hanson, John Gray, Bonnie Ross-Parker, Patricia Fripp and many more. I have learned about the power and motivation that we carry with us every day.

I am of the mindset that we should always be learning or, what Brian Tracy so eloquently calls, *The law of continuous learning.* And Napoleon Hill states, *The mind serves best what is used most.* In 12 years of corporate training, I have trained senior sales personnel to grow personally and professionally with daily education. In today's ever-changing and fast-paced world, personal and professional development training is a requirement for anyone wanting to increase their earning potential. We are experiencing a paradigm shift in how, when and where we get our education. Colleges today have recognized the opportunity in offering online education. After a college graduates enter the workforce, time and money may not be available to attend training. With companies tightening budgets, many aren't willing to invest in training. Therefore, we each have to 'own' our destiny and take time on a daily basis to continue stimulating our brains and help grow in our careers as well as in our personal lives.

Many top people shared that they learned from others in their fields and modeled what successful people have achieved to become experts. We all need to strive to achieve more prosperity, deepen our relationships and attain a higher level of success *through education*. We have entered the information age, and education is more important than ever! Ask yourself what your Entertainment vs. Education (EvE) ratio is. Did you know that if you spend 15 minutes a day educating and training yourself then in one month you would have eight hours of training and in one year you would have 12 days of training? People spend millions of dollars on books, CDs, DVDs, seminars, conferences, etc. We need to become part of a knowledge-based society.

I have had the privilege of being trained under many of the best in the industry. Unfortunately, downsizing has affected many talented individuals and they are not able to continue this training. We need to have this opportunity whether we are baby boomers or just graduating from college. It's critical to our development.

In the end, I was introduced to a new personal and professional development concept in online training with world-class experts and now am able to learn from the best daily. This has resulted in a more positive environment for my career as well as my personal life. Having access to world renowned leaders in their field of expertise delivered in short 8–12 minute sound bites of relevant content and the ability to apply immediately in your daily life. The content ranges from leadership, communication, starting your business, life balance, letting go, tax strategies and much more. There is also content available for teens! Everyone has access so please contact Vicki as she would love to share more information with you.

Investing in yourself helps you connect to others. Your interests and abilities give you topics to discuss with people you meet. By learning new skills or strengthening your current skills you become more confident. Helping people grow and achieve their dreams is the fastest route to success—both theirs and yours. To success!

# 12

## Be In Contribution To Others

**Anne Alberg**

**Actively listen to determine how you can contribute to others.**

Zig Ziglar said it best: *You can have everything in life you want, if you will just help other people get what they want.*

I have always been naturally curious to learn about other people. When I first meet someone, I ask questions to determine how I might be able to assist them. Questions might include what they do, what they are passionate about, whether they face any business challenges, etc. Not only does this help me establish rapport, I am able to determine if I have something that will help them or if I know of a resource for them. Often, I am able to immediately connect them to someone who has what they are looking for.

The result—I now connect two people who might not have otherwise discovered each other. Many times, people then ask how they can assist me. As is human nature, they are now more motivated to find a way to reciprocate in helping me find what I am looking for.

As J.T. O'Donnell says, "It's not what you know. It's who knows you!" By being a resource and making connections for others, I have become known as the "Networking Diva." People know to reach out to ask if I know who can help them. This creates 'Top of Mind' awareness for me and my business. Along the way, they become advocates for what I do. Then when someone asks, *Do you know...,* my advocates say, *You need to call Anne Alberg.*

Networking by being in contribution to others has recently become even easier online with the expanded use of online social networking communities. I can now reach out to two people whom I think should know about each other, and initiate a connection between them. This allows me to gently keep in touch and deepen our relationships.

How can you apply the concept of Successful Networking through Contribution?

- Create a list of 2–3 questions you can ask someone when you first meet them. Specifically ask them about the one thing they are looking for that would make a difference in their business or take them to the next level.
- Actively listen to determine how you can be in contribution to them.
- Take notes on the back of their business card so you can remember what they are looking for. Include the date and the name of the event where you met them.
- Respond in the next 24–48 hours if you promised to send them an email.
- If you made a good connection or if you may want to follow up with them at a later date, immediately enter them into your contact management database.
- As you discover ways to be in contribution, reach out to them via the phone or email. In affect, you are being their advocate as you make connections for them.
- Along the way, educate them on what you are looking for so they can be in contribution to you.

**30-Day Challenge:** Take five minutes each morning to review the profiles on one of your social networking sites or think of someone you know that you can be in contribution to that day. This could be making a connection for them, using their service or giving them a marketing idea. Practice being in contribution every day for 30 days and you will see the difference it will make not only in your business, but also in your personal life.

# 13 Network With Enthusiasm

### Susan Hendrix

**The most enthusiastic networkers have a genuine passion and belief in their product or business.**

*It's faith in something and enthusiasm for something that makes a life worth living.*
- Oliver Wendell Holmes

I love people. I love meeting them, socializing with them, helping them and experiencing everything that comes with human interaction. Over the years I have also enjoyed doing a huge amount of networking. When meeting lots of people at any event, who are you most likely to remember? Who do you most enjoy talking with? Who do you want to support? Yes...the most enthusiastic people are networking magnets! They 'draw' you to them, and they are the ones you remember best!

The most enthusiastic networkers have a genuine passion and belief in their product or business. When you are truly 'in love' with your job, it is easy to be enthusiastic and it is easy to share your enthusiasm with others. It is like you have an inner sun that effortlessly radiates to others.

Do you have that passion and belief in what you are doing? If not, go back to when you first joined your company or started your business. What was your 'why?' Make a list of the benefits you are providing to others. How has your business changed your life and the lives of others? Rekindle that passion, and your enthusiasm will increase and flow naturally. Being passionate about something gives you boundless energy and a strong desire to succeed. It gives you the ability to outlast any obstacles that come your way. You can keep your focus on your end goal if you have that firm belief in yourself and what you are doing. I remember the analogy of driving in your car—how you must focus on the road ahead and not on the bugs on the windshield. If you start looking at the bugs while you are driving you are not going to make it to your destination. If you cannot be enthusiastic about networking, find something you can be passionate about! "It's faith in something and enthusiasm for something that makes a life worth living."

Are you also excited about learning more about the people you meet? Have you heard the acronym FAYC—Forget About Yourself Completely? One great question to ask is, "What do you love about what you do?" It is fun to observe how individuals sometimes have to stop and think about this question, and how they then immediately brighten up as they describe their passion. They in turn will remember that you cared enough to ask. People don't care how much you know until they know how much you care. Networking is fun and productive when you make it "not about yourself or what you can gain from those you network with," but truly about the people you are meeting.

When I think of enthusiastic networkers, one dynamic woman comes to mind instantly. She is a third-generation financial planner and speaks with great pride in continuing this legacy. Her eyes sparkle as she offers to be the GPS of your finances, getting you from where you are now to where you want to be. Her knowledge is powerful, but her enthusiasm for what could be a very dry subject is the key to her success. I have observed how she always asks questions to learn more about the people she is talking to. Because of her love for what she does, she gains trust, and people are willing to share very personal information about their finances. It is not surprising that most of her leads come from networking!

She is an enthusiastic networking magnet and you can be too!

# 14 | Keep In Touch

**Annette S. Walden**

**Annette S. Walden**

**I would never have to go to the card store again.**

I have always enjoyed sending greeting cards, especially birthday cards, to all of my family, friends and business clients. It is my way of keeping in touch with people I care about since I'm not much for picking up the phone and calling someone. I would go to the greeting card store with my list and spend hours picking out just the right card. Not only did the card have to have just the right verse, but, because of my love of butterflies, I also wanted it to have a butterfly on it. Even though I made the trip to the card store quite frequently, I still would find myself needing a card for an occasion and not having it on hand, especially get-well and sympathy cards. Then I would get aggravated when I didn't have the time to go to the store. Alas, a couple of weeks would go by, and I still had not sent that all-important card, one which was really more important than a birthday card.

One day in my search for material on 'The Laws of Attraction,' I came across a tag line beneath a person's name that invited me to send a free greeting card. Okay, I was all into sending cards. So I tried it. Wow, was I ever impressed! This was an online service that I could use anytime—I could personalize my card any way I wished, and the company would print my card and mail it for me. I would never have to go to the card store again. *Sign me up!* Now I could send all my cards in a timely fashion.

My plan was to use the service for personal use and for my other business. I soon found myself sharing this wonderful service with all my friends, family, and business acquaintances. I soon saw the value and changed my business focus to relationship marketing because I truly believe any business will grow and flourish by building the relationships with clients first.

Through my keeping in touch with friends, family, and clients even more using my SendOutCards service, my business grew tremendously. What I found amazing is that my business continues to grow as my greeting cards clients use the system. Their recipients of the cards like the cards so much, that they want to know about the service also.

One story is about an organizer who spoke at a local conference and received a thank-you card from my client. She was so impressed with the card that she tried the service herself and soon signed herself up for a wholesale account. Another client who has a vending machine company wrote me an amazing testimonial about how he had procrastinated after signing up for the service and finally sat down and sent 42 cards in no time at all using the service. My best success story is of a realtor who told me the first time I spoke to her about the cards. She didn't think she needed the service because she could go to the dollar store and get her cards for fifty cents. On the urging of her husband, who told me to call her again, she signed up because she realized she had not been to the store to get any cards and had not sent any cards in several months. She just recently won a cruise due to her marketing of her SendOutCards business.

It is truly satisfying to be doing what you love to do and be financially rewarded for it also. Even more rewarding is being able to share this wonderful service with others and see their business grow as a result of it. To have them come back to me and thank me for sharing this wonderful service makes my mission of 'Keeping in Touch' even more special.

# 15

# Make Real Connections Online

### Debbie Baus

**You definitely can forge worthwhile and valuable real-world connections in the online world.**

The Internet is so broad and vast, with so many places and people, that it can seem terribly impersonal. What connections can you really form without ever meeting someone? Well, you definitely can form significant connections, if you keep a few things in mind.

In my case, I have a daughter with Kabuki Syndrome. Ever heard of it? Probably not. It's a rare genetic disorder. So rare that the number of diagnosed cases in the world numbers only in the hundreds. Think there were any local parents' groups when she was diagnosed? Not! I immediately turned to the Internet and discovered the Kabuki Support Network, a network of parents all over the world who connect, primarily through a standard Yahoo! Group, and exchange stories of medical issues, learning problems, family dysfunction, and so much more. That online support group has been a critical part of my daughter's care. The connections I've formed online, rarely meeting face-to-face, have led to heart-to-heart exchanges I haven't had within my real-world circles because no one else shares the connection of having a child with Kabuki like that online group. Now that's real-world connection online!

However, real connections must follow certain guidelines. For example:

**Be authentic.** No connection, real-world or online, will be real if you're faking it. Since it's so easy to become someone you're not online, you might be tempted to fudge the facts here and there. If you do, you're totally wasting your time. Don't be afraid to use your real name. Don't be afraid to relate your real experiences. The more authentic you are and the more of yourself you put into the connection, the more real it will be.

**Be sincere.** Just like in the real world, online acquaintances can typically see through fake concern and praise. Being sincere online requires answering emails all the time instead of just when you want to send a marketing message. It requires giving value without expectations of repayment every time. Obviously, if you provide a service, you charge for it, but it works best to give friendly advice to build goodwill among your connections, just like in real-world networking.

**Invest your time.** Making connections, real-world or online, typically takes more than one interaction. If you sincerely want to make connections within an online community, you have to stay current and make timely comments and responses. The other option is to jump in, leave some marketing message, and never return, which is a waste of the little bit of time required to do it—so why bother? Take part in the online conversation by reading to find out what's being discussed and then taking time to leave worthwhile comments.

**Take a time out.** This is probably the best tip: contain your knee-jerk reaction by giving yourself a cooling off period before responding to something that gets you hot under the collar. Too often, written words, without the benefit of tone and inflection, can be taken wrongly. Give your connections the benefit of the doubt. If you're offended, take time to cool off and analyze the exchange before writing a logical and mutually beneficial response.

The Internet is a big place. As such, it offers millions of potential connections. By carefully choosing your online communities, being careful not to spread yourself too thin at any one time, and investing yourself as well as your time, you definitely can forge worthwhile and valuable real-world connections in the online world.

# 16 Keep Kindness Alive

**Kathy Greider**

**Always give a person a chance to prove themselves—they may not know what good is inside them until they need to find it.**

*Three things in human life are important: The first is to be kind. The second is to be kind. The third is to be kind.*
- William James

Growing up I had two outstanding women who mentored me—my mom and my grandma. They taught me by example never by preaching to me. I am going to tell you about the lessons learned from my grandma who connected people everyday with her generosity and kindness.

Early in childhood, I had a conversation with Grandma. I asked her why so many people came to her for help. I was afraid of some of the men who came to meet her (they weren't always as clean as I thought they should be). She said they were just down on their luck and needed someone. Grandma told me—*always give a person a chance to prove themselves—they may not know what good is inside them until they need to find it.* She always found work for the men even if they had to mow a lawn that didn't really need to be mowed. She would pay them, feed them and send food home to their families. By being respectful to the people that came to her back door in the same way she was respectful to her friends who came to the front door, she gained widespread respect. Years later at her funeral I saw many of those same people come to pay their last respects—everyone loved her.

If you treat people with kindness you receive that kindness back in kind. As an example, recently I returned my rental car at the airport. The line was long—not because the attendants were slow but because there were not enough of them. The man ahead of me complained about the extra wait. When the attendant approached me he started to apologize for the delay; I simply stated, "no problem—looks like you are shorthanded." He smiled and said, "yes that's true—thanks." Then he asked me whether my car was okay. I told him, "Yes, but even though it was a non-smoking car someone had smoked and it didn't smell good." I was making a comment—not a complaint. He graciously took back my bill and reduced my total by 20%! We were kind to each other and showed empathy and sympathy—and both won.

There are many examples I could use to illustrate how kindness brings us together in the networking world—spending a bit more time with someone new to networking, taking the time to introduce the newbie to a few people you know they should know, contacting them after you've met to follow up—all this takes time, but think how great you've just made that new person feel. They will remember you and your kindness will come back to you many times over.

Recently some of my Joy of Connecting attendees, who are in between jobs, were looking for a support group with women in similar circumstances. They asked me for help in getting a group started. We came up with a name—*Our Next Act—A Networking Support Group for Women Seeking Employment.* Our goal is to offer support, encouragement, and answers to the many questions women have regarding unemployment. We meet every week. Sometimes we have a speaker, at other times we just talk. We have created a resource list, a job board, a *Linkedin group* and even helped find a job for one of our members. The group is working well because we are meeting a need—our members feel better about themselves. I have made new friends and have been invited to speak to 850 people about to lose their jobs. This is an outstanding opportunity for me because one of my specialties is personal search optimization—the exposure will be fantastic. I would never have received the invitation if I had not started the group.

*Kindness Connects—Grandma was right!*

# 17

# Lead With Your Magnificence

**Karen Stone**

**Remember you are not creating something new—you are connecting to something that already exists!**

Several years ago, a wise and marketing-savvy friend suggested that my business would be more successful if I branded myself. I had heard this before (several times, in fact) and yet I resisted putting who I am in a box with a title on it. This particular day, I was a bit more open-minded than usual. So, I decided to expand my perspective of branding and do some research.

Instead of going to the Internet, I went to people who know me well: clients, friends, business associates, and the receptionist at my hair salon. I asked them one question: What is it that connects us to each other?

I found out something that I knew intuitively, but had not yet attempted to put down on paper. Here are the results: People 'get' that I see and believe in their unique magnificence. And because of this, they feel good when we connect. And guess what? So do I!

The connecting point has nothing to do with a product or service, a catchy phrase or a special offer. It is all about the energy that is exchanged by two people. True connection starts with how we *each feel* in the presence of the other.

Yet, we often overlook this. Many of us have a default 'on' mode that steps up to the plate when we walk into a networking situation. We may feel we need to dazzle or impress others. We may unconsciously switch from being who we *are* to being who we *think we should be* in order to connect.

If this happens, we have just pushed our biggest asset into the background. We have dimmed the most valuable of all connections—the direct connection to our own magnificence. We have taken our unique lead and buried it in small print in chapter five of our energy exchange.

So how do we bring our connection to our magnificence out of the shadows and lead with it? Here are some tips and tools that work for me.

- Acknowledge that you are unique. You are magnificent. Period.
- Remember you are not creating something new—you are connecting to something that already exists! (That would be your magnificence!)
- Before you put your energy 'out there,' focus your energy inward. Consciously connect with your magnificence.
- Imagine a time in your life when you knew you were in the exact right place, at the exact right time, doing the right and perfect thing. This is what being connected to your magnificence feels like!
- Experiment and design your own unique way of connecting with your magnificence.
- Give your magnificence permission to be present!
- When you meet someone, silently offer your magnificence to them in service to their magnificence. Come up with a phrase that you say in your head when you first look into someone's eyes. Mine is, "The magnificence in me greets the magnificence in you."

Now, here is the best part. When you lead with your magnificence, the other person's magnificence cannot help but peak out! Your new connection begins on a very empowering note—magnificence to magnificence.

And guess what else happens? When someone reconnects with their magnificence in your presence, they remember you. Not because you offered them the best product since sliced bread, but because you happened to be there when they found that spark of magnificence in themselves that may have been smoldering.

Connect with your own magnificence and you will connect meaningfully with others and their magnificence. It is *you*, not the product or service that you offer, that makes the difference in someone's life. And, here's a bonus. Every time you lead with your magnificence, you nurture the most valuable, honest connection you have—the one with the magnificence that you naturally and uniquely are—and it shows up more often.

How's that for a win-win?

# 18 Personalize Your Follow-up

**Phyllis Wallace**

**I take an inventory of who someone is personally and professionally.**

In my life's journey I have always been attracted to work that connects to and serves people. Before and during college I held jobs as a babysitter, jewelry seller, fast food worker, drug store clerk, crisis center worker, book factory worker, paper girl, library attendant, café worker, state employee, truck stop worker and phone survey worker. In college I studied Psychology and ultimately ended up working in Human Resources. While working in Human Resources for Fortune 500 companies people have always said things to me like, "I always feel better after speaking with you," "You make me feel special," "You were an angel to my husband," "Thank you for helping me achieve my goals."

In fact, I have coached everyone from the mailroom to the boardroom. Outside of work I have always encouraged and developed others as a care group leader, friend, counselor, aunt, and godmother. I am intrigued by people's life stories. I have had the honor of working with individuals who have ambitious goals and are open to exploring ways to achieve them. I take an inventory of who they are personally and professionally; we set up a tailored plan for them and have regular check-ins. They accomplish their dreams and I am allowed to participate in their transformed lives.

As I have begun to more closely align my passion with my profession, I have been drawn to work that allows me to fully unleash my gifts and talents for connecting with people in a real and authentic way. In February 2009, I decided to become a licensee for The Joy of Connecting®, a women's networking group. Instantly I began to receive positive feedback on my follow-up. As I think back, there has always been a common theme to my effectively connecting with people—that is how I personalize my follow-up.

I am excited to share with you three steps to personalize your follow-up for greater success in business and life:

**Be present in the initial face-to-face conversation.** Look the person in the eye. Smile, be attentive and ask questions about the person and their business. Look for the light in their eye to figure out what is important to them. Take notes!

**Send a follow-up communication by mail or make a phone call to thank them for their time.** Be sure to mention a phrase or something they said that made their eyes sparkle. Let them know you look forward to partnering with them.

**Add something about yourself that is uniquely you.** For example, I have been told that my positive thoughts, open and honest sharing boosts emotional energy. Find out and leverage what is special about you and then use it!

Through this method I have been able to successfully launch my Joy of Connecting Networking group and in January 2008 I was named to the Founding Leaders Circle of Honor as an Independent Consultant for Blessings Unlimited.

# 19 Share From Your Heart

Dr. Linda Katz

**When your heart is open, people know not only by your words but also by your actions.**

When connecting with others I let my heart direct me. I feel each person has something to say that will enrich my life. This enrichment enables me to pass on the connections and share it with others. It is a choice to listen, to participate and learn what helps each of us to connect. When your heart is open, people know not only by your words but also by your actions. They can feel that you care and because of this they choose to allow you into their lives. They want to share with you thereby creating a connection.

You choose the energy level that exists between two people meeting for the first time. Energy, excitement, enthusiasm and a smile are sure ways to attract others to you. You create your life and the choices you make, so choose to make every connection a strong and positive one. Having a great attitude and being grateful for what you have brings blessings into your life. Being happy isn't a function of your circumstances; it is a function of your attitude.

I have always had a great attitude and choose to have a sunny disposition to get me through everything that life throws my way. When my daughter was born with brain injury I could have allowed my circumstances to dictate my emotions. It would have been very easy to have a "Why me?" attitude. Instead, my attitude was "How do I fix it?" I decided to find out what she could and could not do. I then became determined to create a wonderful life for us. When you choose your attitude and response to your circumstances you make decisions, take action and take control.

In my profession as a chiropractor, I have people come in with complaints about aches and pains. It is my job to turn those around into solutions for a healthier life. Complaining is a negative choice and does not enhance problem solving, rather it repels it. Sometimes we are reluctant to open ourselves up and share our heart with others. By sharing my concern, enthusiasm and goals for their health, it helps them to understand someone cares and wants the best for them. I have found this is a rare find for some people. Surrounding yourself with those who care only enhances your ability to communicate feelings and make great connections.

Having a sunny disposition has enhanced my life. I'm nicknamed 'the Energizer bunny,' due to the excitement and energy I bring to each unique situation. My attitude and genuine care for people have a positive affect on the lives of others around me. They are more willing to open up and share their true wants and desires with me.

*How is your attitude?* Are you letting your circumstances close your heart and closing your chances for connections? Remember, it is easier to ride a roller coaster than to drag it behind you. By keeping a good attitude, and always looking forward, you will find an opportunity to make connections. Choose to have an attitude that will reflect the inner feelings of your heart. When you connect from the heart true feelings are shared, that is what connecting is about.

# 20

# Honor Gender Differences

**Lori Finlay-Hamilton**

**Understanding gender differences has opened up a whole new world of possibilities in connecting, communicating and partnering.**

As a young woman, my career was focused in connecting and relating to mostly women. I was a young nurse and initially needed to connect and develop relationships with my fellow nursing colleagues—mostly women. I found it easy to relate and get along with women yet found it more difficult to develop professional relationships with my male colleagues, often physicians. I became a nurse practitioner and enjoyed more of a collegial relationship with the medical staff. I found that understanding and honoring gender differences was even more critical. I had to understand how to get to the point and provide critical information for my colleagues and I to make informed decisions. Understanding gender differences has opened up a whole new world of possibilities in connecting, communicating and partnering.

Over the past few years I have researched, enrolled in courses and read many books on the subject of gender differences. Two excellent books are 'Why Men Never Remember and Women Never Forget' by Marianne J. Legato, M.D. and 'The Female Brain' by Louann Brizendine, M.D. I found that men were genetically designed to be hunters, singularly focused—producing one result after another (imagine slaying the dragon in caveman days) hour after hour, day after day. To accomplish this successfully, they were engineered perfectly!

The data or information that men are listening for is all related to producing the best result, the fastest. Men are listening for:

- Methods - the best ways to produce the result
- Terrain - where to get what is needed to succeed
- Alliances - or who to have on his team to ensure success
- Strengths and weaknesses - of himself, his teammates and "the animal" he is hunting
- Statistics - the facts that will define the likelihood of him winning or losing

Women on the other hand were genetically designed to be the gatherers. Thus women also have specific information they are gathering and listening for to enhance communication. Mind you, today's modern world women find themselves, especially in the work force, learning and even emulating, many of the character traits described for men. Women want to know:

- Time and location—they will remember these critical details and share in a conversation.
- Specific features that distinguish one item from another—just think how a woman knows which specific brand of an item she wants at the grocery store.
- A series of very specific processes, in a specific order (this can be different for all women too).

Now, let's translate this to our professional lives and to making connections. A few years ago, I was working with an international organization and had met the new Executive VP of Global Sales/Marketing. There was an initiative or project that I was passionate about that was very important to hundreds, even thousands of female colleagues. However, the decision had already been made that they were not going forward. In connecting with this new VP, I needed to first listen for what was important to him. His job/result was to make the marketing dollars and projects give the biggest bang for the buck. Instead of being offended that he did not feel this project was of value, I was able to listen and honor his thoughts and objectives, thus getting our relationship off to a great start. We selected a time to discuss the project and after presenting the information that he was looking for how this project would align with his vision and objectives of winning he turned a *no*, into a *yes*! And the project rolled forward changing everything!

When I meet someone today, I listen to the questions and answers much more closely. It's pretty easy to know if speaking with a man what information will enhance our connection—yet with a woman, again, it can be a bit tricky. Carefully listening, will help you find out if she is in hunter mode and up to producing a big result, or if she is now in casual girlfriend conversations, sharing all the details of her day. These simple tips have turned meetings into connections and fostered valuable relationships, partnerships less stress and more success!

# Think You Can

**Heather Doering**

**What if goal setting became an assumed part of life?**

Much of our day-to-day existence is driven by habit: wake up, grab the morning coffee, exercise, get dressed, etc. We accomplish everyday tasks simply because we expect to. They're an assumed part of life.

What if goal setting became an assumed part of life? We'd expect to achieve our goals, because accomplishing goals would become habit. I recently accepted a challenge to meet some aggressive goals with SimplyFun. I committed to holding 20 parties, sponsoring five people into the company, and selling at least $6000 of product in ten weeks. I'd never done anything even remotely close to those numbers. I decided early on that failure was not an option I was willing to entertain, which meant I needed to figure out how to accomplish those three goals, and do it fast!

Ten weeks, three major goals. So much to do in so little time! I needed a plan, so I talked with my manager. She encouraged me to break each goal down into weekly and then daily mini-goals. I recruited mentors to encourage me and hold me accountable to the tasks before me. I worked really hard, even when my goals seemed to be slipping away. I came really, really close, and then gave up. My encouragers, however, didn't give up on me, and we (yes we, since I'd given up and they hadn't), made it to the finish line.

Until I met that challenge, my attitude was that goal setting was fine for others, if stuff like that motivated them. I'd set my goals, and say "I *think* I can." My goals were flexible—if I don't make it, that's okay; I tried and should be proud of my efforts; I'll lower my expectations and goals to fit my fears; I can change the goal when it gets too tough, right? *Wrong!* Goals aren't fluid. They are measurable, tangible, and motivating. Goals are personal, keep us focused on the prize, and are finite. Sometimes we fall short, but more often than not, we *succeed*, simply because we committed to success!

Achieving that challenge changed my life. I no longer accept less than my best. I realized I can do anything I put my mind to. Goals now rule my life—my job, my JOC events, even my wellness.

I recently saw myself in some pictures and was less than thrilled with my chubby appearance. I'd been trying to shed those baby pounds for years, but to no avail. I decided I *had* to lose weight, set a goal to lose 20 pounds, created a support network, and did it. It wasn't easy, it wasn't always exciting, and my modified eating must become habit for me to keep the weight off, but I *did* it. I established a measurable (20 pounds is easy to measure on a scale!), attainable (20 pounds, not 100), tangible (yes, I need to buy new clothes), motivating and finite (my incentive trip to Hawaii is just around the corner) goal and chose to accomplish it. I recruited a partner who followed the same program (support network), and I *did* it!

Stop reading and write down five long-term goals (to be accomplished within the next five years) and five short-term goals (to be accomplished within the next 90 days). Post them in a very visible place—your office, your bathroom mirror, your dashboard. Keep them in your face! Find one or two people to embrace your goals with you, and *let them*! They'll be your cheerleaders, your encouragers, your listeners, your partners.

Goal-setting works, even for skeptics like me. What does this have to do with habits? As you set and achieve goals on a regular basis, goal setting will become habitual. You'll accomplish amazing things in all areas of your life. I *know* you can *do it*!

# Look Beyond The Surface

**Carole McNichol**

I can say that I am a people person, I know it, and people who know me will tell you I am Miss Chatty. It's not that I want to know anyone's business; I just love to meet new interesting folks. My business is a people business. As a financial advisor, I do business with individuals, so I have to network. I need to build relationships. For me, everyone is a prospect. Everyone needs my services no matter how small.

By not pre-judging, but building relationships over time, I scored my biggest single client. Between 1999 and 2000, Carla and I went to the same church and our sons played on the same soccer team. While our kids practiced we would just talk about life on the sidelines and the concerns that mothers and women normally talk about. Carla was a stay-at-home mother who had recently gone through a bad divorce. She had two boys: one in elementary; the other in middle school. Both boys were in a private Christian school. At the time, I was working on my Certified Financial Planner (CFP) designation. Carla had been trained as a Certified Public Accountant (CPA) prior to staying home with her kids.

During our conversations, Carla would always have interesting questions about the stock market. One day Carla asked me to meet her for lunch. This ordinary, conservative investor pulled out her brokerage statements at the restaurant and asked me what I thought. I was surprised that a restaurant was the place she chose to show me that she was a millionaire. After a brief discussion, we agreed for me to do a more in-depth analysis of her portfolio. I was then living in an extended stay hotel, waiting for my son to finish school so we could join my husband in Atlanta. Carla ended with wanting me to manage a portion of her portfolio, even after I mentioned that I was moving from Florida to Atlanta in just weeks. Did this stop the deal? No!

We can also take the example of Susan Boyle, the woman on the recent 'Britain's Got Talent' show who was pre-judged by most. Susan Boyle, a plain 47-year-old woman who said her dream was to be a professional singer, at her own admission had never been kissed. The audience was sneering, and the judges thought she was slightly nuts. The surprise was as soon she opened her mouth and sang like an angel.

So when I meet someone I always engage that person, regardless of who he or she may be, because as I have found in the past you cannot judge a person by his or her appearance. When one is networking, people tend to navigate to the flamboyant people within the room. What I am saying is: consider who may seem reserved. Show interest in that person; you may be surprised by what that person has to offer you.

If you do not judge people by their appearance, and instead build relationships, you may be surprised at the trust you can build. I closed a $600,000 deal with Carla.

# 23 Be The Bearer Of Gifts

**Diana Nichols**

**You possess a wealth of ideas and information that you can gift to others.**

One of the easiest ways to really connect with someone, and make an impression, is to give them a gift that has real value to them.

Notice the last part of the sentence...'value to them.' Many times we give gifts that mostly have value to us—promotional items with our logo on them, business cards, brochures, etc. Occasionally, we give away free samples or coupons. These are good things, but hardly memorable. And most are seen as self-serving.

The gifts I'm referring to are not tangible things, but rather ideas. You possess a wealth of ideas and information that you can gift to others. You know people, you've had many life experiences, and you have knowledge about your business. There's a lot of stuff in your memory bank!

Any marketing guru will tell you that one of your basic tools is a list of tips and techniques that you should share freely. I'll bet you can lay your hands on one or ten such lists right now. This is a great place to start creating your 'gift basket.'

Before you run off to the copy machine to make 1000 copies, let me say that the most effective way to give these away is *one at a time, in one-on-one conversation.* (The conversation can be in person, on the phone, or via email.)

Look over the lists of tips: find a few that are really meaningful, and not as widely known as others. These are the ones you want to use. Memorize and be ready to call them up.

Now, let's add some more gifts to your repertoire. Looking over your 'tips' list, are there any other tidbits that you've learned yourself that have been especially helpful?

How about ideas or techniques you use in other areas of your life? Ways you manage your daily life that perhaps not everyone uses. Bet you have a few of those. They don't have to be your original idea, just things that work for you—or someone you know.

Keep going...

You can add all the people you know well enough to be able to recommend them.

Also, make a list (mental or physical) of the helpful books and articles you've read lately.

Wow, your basket's getting bigger! You have a lot of gifts to share.

And the best part is that now you have created the basket, you'll be on the lookout for new ideas and people to add to it. It will just keep growing!

So what do you do with all these gifts? Look for opportunities to give them away.

When you make a connection, listen carefully to the other person. If you are really paying attention, you will often hear a clear clue as to what you can share that might be valuable to them. If you don't hear a clue, then ask questions.

- What's your biggest challenge right now?
- What would make you more successful?
- How can I help you?

Use your own words, and be sincere. Even if you still can't find anything really pertinent to give, at the very least you have given them the gift of caring enough to ask!

Just a few words about sharing your personal knowledge and experiences. The value in your experience for someone else is not the "story" about it. The who, where, how, and why are only relevant to you. It's in the *what* that the value lies for them. Just the facts, Ma'am. Share the lesson learned, the result, the essence. Make it short and to the point.

And finally, make sure your gift sounds like a gift—not like advice: Have you ever thought of...? I've had success with.... Have you read...? Do you know...?

Giving is, after all, the best way to receive!

# 24

# Connections With Aloha

**Wendy Keahi Kirley**

**We all know that sharing is caring...and caring is Aloha!**

Aloha is a word that propels Hawaii, because Aloha, when used appropriately, denotes care. Caring is a significant part of making connections and in Hawaii, a few caring traditions make connecting easier than it might otherwise be.

There's a natural relationship that is created by us all as we address adults older than ourselves as 'Auntie' or 'Uncle,' even though we are not biologically related. It's done out of respect for our elders while at the same time instantly breaking down barriers of formality. We all become Auntie or Uncle to someone at some point. This unites neighborhoods and communities (I'm Auntie Wendy to every child on my block) and encourages each to watch out for and help one another as we would our own family because, by our manner of addressing one another, we are family.

The lei, a garland of flowers, is given to welcome strangers to the islands and is a gift at parting to bid farewell; helping travelers to conjure memories of time spent in a tropical paradise. Lei are also offered for celebrations; a graduate piled high with lei from various family and friends in honor of his or her achievement is a common sight. A lei is a circle of love, friendship, and support; a gift of Aloha.

How many people ask, "How are you?" because they truly want to hear how an individual is? When people in Hawaii gather, it is not unusual for them to 'talk story.' *Talk story* is a good phrase, a broken English or 'Pidgin English' phrase, meaning *more than a casual chat*. It's not unusual for the participants to lose track of time when engaged in *talking story* as each sincerely seeks to know how the other is doing.

I've lived in Hawaii for most of my life and am of part-Hawaiian ancestry; therefore, these traditions are a way of life for me and make connecting a natural process because connecting is part of each tradition. One not living in Hawaii may not feel comfortable with initiating any of the practices of the islands toward making connections. But all can still take a few cues from these Hawaiian traditions.

People of all walks of life are generally seeking the same thing: to be acknowledged and accepted in spite of differences while making a difference in and leaving their mark on the world. Taking the time to learn how another prefers to be addressed offers respect. All relationships start with respect, which creates comfort, enables one to relax, and encourages a desire to assist and reciprocate.

A circle of fresh flowers is not always possible or practical, but another tradition in Hawaii is easily given: a circle of arms around another person; a hug. Everyone hugs in Hawaii on first meetings. The manner in which that greeting is presented reveals how the giver and recipient are feeling about this interaction. Whether nervous, uncomfortable, tense, or open, it's all revealed in a hug. Not a hugger? How about a circle of a hand around another's; a handshake? A firm handshake shows confidence, but can also share warmth and strength. Whichever method is used, it is touch that can warm hearts and will be remembered longer than words.

'Talking story' takes time. But making connections takes time. It's really about consideration and genuine concern. A common courtesy would be to ask what another's time frame is like so you will know what your *story time* will amount to. Unlike story time at the public library or book store that is more of a recitation, 'talking story' means that each takes turns exchanging ideas and sharing thoughts about what matters most to each at that time.

We all know that sharing is caring...and caring is Aloha! Live Aloha wherever you are and find yourself more easily making lasting impressions and connections!

# Live In The Now With Empathy

**Caroline Scranton Bell**

Sometimes, the cruelest twist of fate turns into the catalyst for a chrysalis and birth of better things when handled with empathy and caring.

After 18 years in corporate America, I was totally caught off guard and devastated when my world changed overnight—a few times over. My journey "From Living in the Future to Living in the Now with Empathy" began on June 6th of 2006, when I was laid off from my high-level executive job. In one month I lost my position with the company I felt married to, and then my sister and I learned that our mother had severe dementia and that we needed to bring our parents into our homes. So I went from being a corporate executive to being a caregiver to my 84-year-old father. I realized I could not go back and work in corporate America because I would be trading my salary to his hired caregiver. What did the words 'caregiver' even mean? Executive to caregiver? Respite care in lieu of vacation? Dementia? It was overwhelming.

I was crushed; I had been working and saving towards my retirement since I was 21. I had plans and was right on target at 50 to live my dream. I thought Mom and Dad had their act together—they ran a successful business, had life insurance and a healthy retirement account and had paid off their house. Did I have to worry about them when I was climbing the corporate ladder to fulfill my dreams? As it turns out, yes, even if I didn't realize it.

I began to help my father, while struggling through my new reality. I found many challenges to knowing which options we had to help our parents. The challenges were tangible—learning how to gain VA benefits, which environment was best for him—living at home or assisted living—and then how to prepare for the chosen environment. Then there's the *emotional aspect*—the struggle of wanting to be there for him, but of also having duties to work, to a spouse, to grown up children and grandchildren. All these considerations are daunting, and taken on at once, as is often the case, quite overwhelming. What I have learned is that all of these and many more decisions need to be made with empathy, *years before* you get the call "Mom has fallen. What do we do now?"

What I originally thought was a burden is now the greatest gift I have been given. To be able to care for my Daddy and have that time with him to learn who I really am is a true blessing. I have connected with my father; and through my empathy, am also launching a business to educate others on how to create an aging plan.

My business, Preparing for Care, LLC, provides much needed education, support and guidance to adult children about to or now caring for their senior parents. We are an information portal, helping people learn (without getting burned) how to choose a place for their parents, plus much more. We are a resource center—for those needing to find reliable, vetted specialized services for their parents. But most of all, we are a safe haven for one of the most trying and emotionally charged situations anyone can face—one for which most of us are simply not prepared. We help others through this frightening ordeal or help them prepare prior to it, with high-class, top-notch, caring, empathetic friends on their side (and on their parents' side) in and before the time of need.

# Eye Contact Is Powerfully Personal

**Carolyn B. McCollum**

Eye contact is essential when making a great connection in any situation. While a firm handshake and a warm smile are important, both are enhanced by eye contact. The eyes are said to be the 'windows of the soul.' A popular song says 'the truth is in the eyes 'cause the eyes don't lie.'

I feel that I have another person's attention when they look in my eyes while speaking to me. The opposite is also true. When I meet or greet someone who shakes my hand or speaks to me while looking elsewhere, I feel like they are just performing the ritual. But when someone greets me while making eye contact, I feel a sincere connection.

Mary Kay Ash, founder of Mary Kay Cosmetics, taught her sales force to treat everyone they meet as if they are wearing an invisible sign that says, "Make me feel special." By example she showed us that looking into a person's eyes when you speak or listen to them, certainly conveys that they are special. I have found that after years of following this practice, it is automatic that I make eye contact when I make a connection.

Even when I cannot shake a person's hand or speak to them, I can acknowledge them or communicate my interest in what the person has to say, through eye contact. Encouragement, excitement, support, concern and joy are just a few of the emotions I have seen in the eyes of people I have connected with. In all my work (and play) connecting on some level with people was and is necessary.

I understand how valuable eye contact is in communicating because of many experiences during my personal and professional travels where language could be a barrier. I have found eye contact is essential to communicating with people who speak or understand little of my language when I speak little or none of their language. During the more than fifteen years that I worked as an international flight attendant, eye contact allowed me to understand and convey important things without words in many instances. I have seen 'please,' 'help' and 'thank-you' communicated in the eyes of numerous individuals who could not speak those words to me and I was able to respond with my eyes.

Even where language is not a barrier, eye contact may be an invaluable communications tool. On one flight that had a bit of turbulence, there was an unusual noise and shaking of the airplane as we were on final approach to landing. I was able to communicate my calm by my eye contact with a first-time flyer who was obviously frightened. She told me upon deplaning that the calm in my eyes reassured her that we were safe despite the noise and turbulence. On many other occasions, I experienced the excitement of novice travelers who watched the safety demonstration closely and made that little extra eye contact with me acknowledging that they trusted we knew what to do in an emergency.

Whether helping an apprehensive first-time flyer to relax, advising a client seeking legal assistance, or bringing out the beauty in a shy woman with a makeover, I have found in every instance, eye contact is essential and adds great positive impact to my words in making an effective connection. It may take a conscious effort for a while to practice eye contact with everyone you connect with, but after a short time of this practice, you will understand and feel why eye contact is essential to making an effective connection.

# Create Unlikely Alliances

**Sheila Pearl**

**Consider forming alliances with the so-called "competition."**

Many business ventures have a natural marriage: wedding planners need florists, for example. Those types of connections are obvious to us. The connections that are not so obvious may yield even more powerful results. Consider the opportunity for a salon owner to host a seminar about 'creating financial security' or a boutique might host a book club or a mortgage broker could sponsor a dog show.

Consider also forming alliances with the so-called 'competition.' Crazy, you say? That's only a perspective. Just imagine that there is room for us all in our field, and that we form 'unlikely alliances' with people who might be perceived as our competitors.

When we get creative *and* get connected, the possibilities are unlimited!

**Betty, Adrian and Mona:** Betty was a specialist in working on women with coarse hair. Adrian was a color and highlight specialist. Both women owned salons in the center of a small town. They shared many of the same friends, and even belonged to the same church. From an outsider's perspective, they would have been great business partners.

Many women who knew both Betty and Adrian were not comfortable picking one salon over the other; so they choose to go to neither salon, in efforts to stay neutral. One day at a local networking event, Betty stood up and announced her support of Adrian's salon: "If you need color and highlights, there is only one place to consider! Adrian is your stylist!"

Both women were in a better position when they were servicing the clients whose needs best matched the service they best provided. The clients who had been avoiding both salons were no longer uncomfortable going to one or the other of the salons; rather, with Betty's announcement, she had given the ladies 'permission' to go to the salon that best served their needs. Subsequently, the two salons even hosted joint spa events, where all the ladies came together. Business increased 30% the first year they supported each other.

Betty also had a close personal friendship with Mona, a local financial planner. As talented as Betty was with her styling tools, she was at a loss with managing her personal finances. She was also hearing from her clients that many were having a hard time with managing their financial affairs.

Mona was financially sound and organized, but her image was in desperate need of a makeover. Both women agreed to share their strengths and booked a half-day dedicated to one another. During this time they shared their mutual connections with each other, and even went as far as to make formal introductions both online and by phone to others who would be instrumental in helping accomplish the goals they had both outlined.

Betty has a balanced checkbook, a new IRA account and a financial game plan and Mona has a new image which has increased her self-confidence. Mona's shift in energy and excitement opened up new opportunities for her.

Is that an exponential 'winning connection?' Indeed!

# Embrace Your Passion

**Andrea Brunache**

**No circumstance should distract anyone from the passion inside of them to succeed.**

A person's passion keeps them directly focused to find people who can help them reach their goals, professionally. Thus, what I call, 'networking.' Passionate networking is, *an outward display of intense eagerness and desire to find the 'right people' that will help you be successful or that you can help be successful.* What will also be expressed, which is core to every business person or entrepreneur, is that in order to obtain this monumental place in one's life, you must consistently *display an outward intensity of eagerness and desire to achieve your goal of ownership successfully.* This outward intensity of eagerness and desire to achieve any goal is simply called, passion! It must be within your very soul.

Here is an example of what can happen when you become a passionate networker. I was invited by a friend to participate on her associate's television show called, "You're On My Heart" hosted by Ms. Duhart. I accepted this invitation to support my friend's effort as a participant in the show. A few weeks after this took place, we met for lunch and she invited me to her fundraiser dinner/trade show as a vendor. I accepted this invitation as well, happy to have the opportunity to showcase my Arbonne Health and Wellness business to gain added exposure. At this 2<sup>nd</sup> event, Ms. Duhart introduced me to the guest speaker, Ms. LeMons. We had a lot in common and Ms. LeMons was very inspirational to me. She also invited me to participate at a 3<sup>rd</sup>

event which was a trade show as well. I'm sure you can see the ripple effect in this. My business contacts were growing into valuable leads. This is the end result you will also find when you network through your passion. For me; it's a precious gift to be able to help others grow and prosper their business, specifically a woman-owned business.

In today's world, where change in the economy may slow things down, we have to be realistic about how every industry can be affected. But I believe networking has remained constant. Here is an excerpt of what CEO, Founder and Publisher of 'The National Networker,' Adam J. Kovitz has said:

**FACT #1:** We are living in tougher, more challenging economic times. Corporations are cutting costs, cutting prices; if it can be cut, it's being cut.

**FACT #2:** It is common knowledge that in today's world of higher unemployment and tougher, leaner times that *networking is key to survival.*

It is understood these financially challenging times can weigh heavily upon us all. However, it feels good to know there are others who can relate. No circumstance should distract anyone from the passion inside of them to succeed. When you understand that a helping hand is necessary; everyone can reach their goals. You will surely want to grab as many hands as possible along the way, but also extend your hand to others to help them. It is important to recognize the positive impact you can have in the life of virtually everyone you meet. This will help you build relationships that will go far. It is extremely important to have a networking support system in place. Every person you form a relationship with is one more person who can help you grow your business.

Your passion can spark passion in someone else and it will never diminish your own when you share it, but will surely increase it within you. Be sure to keep an open heart and mind as you meet others in the path of life. The passion and positive attitude that you express will be like a magnet that attracts people. If you have confidence, and know in your heart what excites you about your business, others will have an interest in what you want to present to them, and you will maintain their attention. Remember, it takes time to create valuable relationships or gain an inner circle of friends and partners. While in a group or at an event, the key to your effectiveness is to meet like-minded individuals so that your passion is expressed naturally and in a genuine way. The positive benefit of passionate networking gives the kind of rewards you feel in your heart the kind 'Money Can't Buy.' Everyone has the ability to network or can be developed when you understand exactly what you are passionate about. You will certainly be remembered for the intense eagerness you display. When you express your heartfelt desires, adapt to change through challenging circumstances, help others, and continuously learn, you will *make networking effective through your passion.*

# The Handshake: Your First Impression

**Lyn-Dee Eldridge**

**Communication through a handshake is very powerful.**

Meeting new people for me is so exciting, but I was finding that when I moved to a new place, it wasn't so easy for people to accept me, I didn't understand why. Where I came from, most everyone loved me. Hmmm...I love people. So I had a talk with myself and I asked myself, "Why is it so hard for me to meet new people and be accepted?" When I moved to New Hampshire five years ago, I had to learn how to communicate with others. I've been told I have a very strong New York dominating personality and I realized I was scaring off more people than I was making new friends. I had to think, what would help gain people's trust in me and be more receptive to me. So I thought long and hard and I finally found the answer! It's the handshake!

*Take Notice if You are Shaking Someone's Hand Properly.*

A handshake can tell a lot about a person and believe it or not there is a right and wrong way of doing something so simple. When you go to shake someone's hand, take notice where your hand is being placed. If your hand is positioned on top this means either you or the person shaking your hand thinks that you are better than them. If you are positioned on the bottom, it means you or the person feels that you are the lesser of the two. Make sure your hands are parallel; this shows that you both are equal. Next step, allow them to grip your hand first, if someone shakes your hand softly, this means you should speak to him or her softly, if it is firm, speak to him or her with more authority. Communication through a handshake is very powerful and it is one of the key elements in getting to know who it is you are speaking with and it is *your* first point of identifying with this person and making yourself known! And one more element to your first met and greet. When introducing yourself, make sure you look at your partner directly in their eyes and maintain constant eye contact. Wandering eyes is a dead giveaway of lack of confidence or respect. I know for me this was the key to now having more friends in a new place and I am associating with more people then ever before. More doors are opening up for me and I am so happy I found a solution to building new relationships! I truly hope this helps you develop the new relationships in your life. And when we meet, please come and shake my hand! I can't wait!

# 30 Date Your Business Partners

### Patti McTier

**The best leads are not passed at the meeting, but afterwards, during the day when your business partner runs across the perfect contact for you.**

Dating your business partners is not a cause for a lawsuit. In fact, if you are not doing it, you are missing out on the most beneficial part of networking groups. You're attending your networking groups religiously; you're on time, dressed to the nines and freshly showered. You have more business cards in your pocket than you could ever possibly need. Okay, stand up, how long do I have? Sixty seconds, ninety, three minutes if they're generous, then you sit back down and listen to everyone else's spiel. The hour is up and you pass around your business cards and exchange leads; now on to your day, right? Wrong! The best leads are not passed at the meeting, but afterwards, during the day when your business partner runs across the perfect contact for you. How does this person know you are such a good fit for their client? Easy, because you have established a relationship with your referring partner.

You have to get to know your referral sources. What makes them tick? What motivates them? What are they looking for in a business partner? Can you trust them and more importantly, do they trust you? Oh my gosh, this is a date! So many of us get caught up in the act of going to meetings and expecting a perfect lead to drop in our laps, but if you do not cultivate relationships with those in your networking group, no one will ever feel comfortable sending you their valued connections.

So, how do you begin? Choose one person a week to go out with for coffee or lunch. At the 'date' discuss yourself and ask general questions about your partner. This meeting will be 90% social and 10% business; you are getting to know your referral source on a personal level. The business aspect will be what a good lead looks like for each of you. If you find that you have good chemistry with this person, meet again. This time you will know what type of person they are, who you think they will get along with, and what you can offer them to help their business grow. Guess what? They will be doing the same for you! The second 'date' is what you have been waiting for. You will receive leads, not just semi-warm, written on a piece of paper at a networking group lead, but an in-depth discussion of why this contact is perfect for you. This person was hand picked for your business by someone who understands you and your business goals.

After the initial dates, keep in touch with your business partners. Phone them at least once a month. Send cards remembering their birthdays or special events. Continue to cultivate your relationship and you will reap the rewards. Remember, you can and should date several business partners at a time. The more people you have in your networking group, the more productive your business will become. You will gain a reputation as a good resource for others thus making you a powerful networker. You've heard the old saying it's not what you know, but who you know. By dating your business partners you will establish a solid network of relationships you can build your business on and knowing who you can count on and who will refer you good business is what dating your partners is all about.

# I Have Never Met a Stranger

**Debbi McCloud**

**The key to connecting and never meeting a stranger is being natural, friendly and genuinely interested in those we speak to.**

There are so many ways to connect with people nowadays especially on the Web with such sites as Twitter, MySpace, LinkedIn, blogging sites and others all showing that people want to connect with others and want you to connect with them. But the best form of connection is an in person connection, meeting face to face. No matter where you go, there will always be people that you don't know whether at a networking event, a party, church or out shopping, etc. How do you break the ice? How can you get everyone you don't know, wanting to get to know you?

Haven't you noticed that people always gravitate towards those they know? Their friends or family members, people whom they feel comfortable with and have something in common with. I've seen this countless times and then I am left standing alone, while others are talking and laughing amongst themselves and a having a grand ole time. Well enough is enough! Over the years I have learned a couple tricks; if you apply them you will have everyone you don't know knowing you!

Here's what I do: When I walk into a room, I survey the room to observe who is there and yes, I check to see if there is anyone there I know. It's just human nature to do so. Then I pick out a couple of individuals whom I want to meet. I first try to make eye contact and smile. Depending on the response I receive I proceed to walk over and extend my hand for a warm handshake and bellow a warm hello and introduce myself.

Depending on where I am, I ask what business they are in or if they are moving here or just visiting. Some sort of small talk helps to put people at ease and causes them to remember me. Therefore, the key to connecting and never meeting a stranger is being natural and friendly and genuinely interested in those we speak to. Be a good listener and don't interrupt. Establish eye contact. Eye contact is viewed as an indication of interest in the person being addressed. *Smile!* More than any other bodily feature, our face expresses how we really feel, therefore a smile tells others that you have a kindly feeling toward them. Show sincere interest in the person, ask tactful, non-prying questions allowing the person to talk about themselves or their business. People love to talk about themselves! Get their contact information and give your contact information to them. It also helps to stand, move and speak in a calm dignified way that gives evidence of composure and self-confidence. Whew, that's a lot to remember!

However, after you have made that initial connection, it's important to keep the momentum going and thus grow your relationship. This can be accomplished in several ways—email, telephone or in person. Personally email is easier for me to use to follow-up. I have found various social networking sites to be a key in making connections. LinkedIn is a personal favorite and I have connected with many former workmates and schoolmates from other states using this site.

Networking events provide another ideal way to practice and hone your connection skills. It certainly won't come automatically but with practice and your big pearly whites showing, you too can say that you have never met a stranger!

# The Power Of Being Genuine

## Nancy Munn

**It's about the things we know as networkers; listening, kindness, acknowledgement and friendliness.**

I've had incidents in my life that I didn't think much of at the time and yet they 'felt' different. Here are two incidents that illustrate the *power of being genuine.*

Many years ago after finishing a business trip in NYC, I was taking a bus home to visit my parents in South Jersey. A female friend/colleague and I boarded a bus at the station in NYC. I was in a particularly good mood because it was Friday and I was going home for the weekend, and so I greeted the bus driver with a big smile and said, "Hi, how are you today?" He grumbled something as my friend and I proceeded to our seats at the back of the bus. Before I knew it, the bus driver was standing in front of me at my seat and for a moment I thought something was wrong. It seemed odd that the driver had followed us to our seats and left the bus door unattended as others were boarding. Nothing was wrong. He said hello to me and something to the effect of "you should have told me, I would have given you a free ticket." Then he went back up front to the driver's seat.

My friend and I were dumbfounded. It came out of the blue. (I still don't know what I should have told him; I didn't know him). I simply greeted the driver in a friendly manner and you might have thought I handed him a million dollars! Ah, the *power of being genuine.* Now, mind you I am normally a friendly, outgoing person, but I have my moods. Greeting him this way was not pre-planned or forced. It was natural and it was genuine. The simple act of greeting someone who must see thousands of people in a week on his bus route revealed the power. I didn't connect it then that simply being genuine and acknowledging someone else in such a small way could go so far!

While out to breakfast, I commented on our waitress's beautiful earrings and we had a very brief conversation about their origin. Not thinking anything of it other then being genuinely interested in what she had to say I was shocked when she brought my food to me and whispered that she had given me a free Danish! This is crazy, the power of it all! Free Danish! Free bus ticket in New York City! I'm onto something!

It's the *power of being genuine*! We all have the power within us! It's no trick or secret. It is not premeditated. When you receive a positive reaction to your positive action or an unsolicited, unexpected reciprocation that's when you know you are genuine. Are genuine acts always reciprocated? No, but you can feel their power still. You will know it when you have touched someone. It's all about being genuinely interested in other people. It's about approaching life with a happy face! It's about the things we know as networkers; listening, kindness, acknowledgement and friendliness. It can be as easy as breathing. It's a choice. You can choose to live your life this way. It's understanding the power and using it in an authentic way. It must never be faked. It must never be a means to an end. Make it fun, make it light. Be yourself. Enjoy and be interested in others and they will return the favor.

# 33 Make Consistency a Habit

## Michelle Martin

**Each time you 'touch' your connections, they are that much more likely to think of you when they have a need for what you offer.**

As a business owner, consistency is important, whether you are branding your name by offering services to others, or you are promoting a product someone needs. Make consistency a habit with your connections—when attending networking events, sending emails, mailing a note, or following up with prospects. It is an essential part of creating a business your customers feel confident about.

Keeping your name or brand in front of your connections consistently gives them the opportunity to learn more about you, your products or services, and your organization. Each time you 'touch' your connections, they are that much more likely to think of you when they have a need for what you offer. They will also have a better understanding of what you are looking for, and refer business to you when one of their contacts has a need that you can fulfill.

Since 2004 I have been the publisher of 'Metro Woman,' a woman's guide to businesses in Fort Worth and the surrounding areas, and a member of several different organizations for business-women and local chambers. When visiting a new organization, I consistently attend 3–4 events to get a good idea of whether the people attending the events are from our target market for 'Metro Woman.' I don't join an organization unless I can commit to attending its events consistently. I have found that consistently attending events of the organizations to which I belong provides the best return on both my time and financial investment.

People are drawn to others when they are reliable and consistent in their marketing efforts—it provides a higher level of confidence in your abilities and your business when you are reliable and consistent. For example, if you send a monthly email newsletter to your connections with valuable, useful information, they will come to expect that newsletter in their inbox each month. The same is true of sales, promotions, and events. You might be thinking that you don't have time to be a 'consistent connector' with each of your contacts. However, I can tell you that it is not as difficult as you think, you just need a few systems in place to help you consistency a habit. Once you have a plan, you will be able to stay in touch with your contacts efficiently and effectively. Try the following business tools to get you started:

**Constant Contact** - email marketing service that allows you to send promotions, invitations, and eNewsletters to a large number of contacts at once, http://www.ConstantContact.com.

**Send Out Cards** - a greeting card service that allows you to send a thank you, birthday, or anniversary card and others. You create a card online, and Send Out Cards mails an actual stamped card to your contact, http://www.SendOutCards.com.

**Hire a Virtual Assistant** - hiring a virtual assistant to build your database, and maintain a schedule of how you will consistently 'touch' you contacts is another great way to make consistency a habit. You can find numerous virtual assistants through an online search, or through local business organizations, http://www.VirtualAssistanceU.com or http://www.ivaa.org.

By following these simple guidelines and staying in touch with connections made during networking events, expos, and prospects who call 'Metro Woman' directly, I have built a database of nearly 2,500 subscribers that is used for email marketing. I was also recently recognized as a Constant Contact All Star, a group of Constant Contact users who set a great example for other email marketers by maintaining sound permission-based email marketing and list management practices.

Building a business through making consistency a habit has enriched my life by allowing me to maintain and build relationships with the business owners I come into contact regularly. In turn, my connections know they can depend on and call on me when they need assistance for their own business. I hope you'll take steps to make consistency a habit as well!

# 34 Be Confident In Yourself

**Nancy Hayssen**

For the past 10 years I've received through my website thousands of letters from young girls, women and even men. The most common question over the years still remains the same, "How can I build my own self-confidence so I feel beautiful when connecting with others?"

What does it really mean to be confident? And what are ways that anybody can have a strong sense of confidence, the same type a model has to increase her own self-confidence?

There are three steps to being confident:

**Know yourself**
Ask yourself: Who am I? What traits do I truly like about myself? What do other people love about me? What even bugs people about me? To find out the answers to these questions, you need to be brutally honest with yourself.

Write down five qualities you like about yourself. For example, being determined, kind, adventurous, loyal or creative. Then write down one quality you want to improve. Maybe you want to be a better listener, be more easy-going or gain more patience. Make the qualities unique to *you*.

**Know what you want**
How do you figure out what you really want? It seems sometimes there are so many options to choose from, so where do you start to get clear? To know what you want, you must first get very, *very* specific.

Ask yourself these three questions (in this order): What would I do if I weren't afraid? What would I do with my life if money were no object? What would be better than what I am doing or have now?

These three questions will help you connect to your inner self to free you on an emotional level so you can see your *real* desires. Once you get clear and know exactly what you want, you can then go after it!

## Take inspired action

As easy as this last step seems, for most people it's the hardest. People will get 'analysis paralysis' by letting fear sneak in, analyze all the reasons why they shouldn't do what they need to do and make excuses to not take action.

As confident as I believe myself to be, this once happened to me. I was asked to walk a runway show for a red carpet event in Los Angeles. Since my background in modeling was limited to print work, this was a stretch. But I told myself I could do it.

When it came time for the actual live event, I literally froze at the foot of the runway. "What if I stumble and fall?", "What if I look ridiculous?", "What if my clothes fall off?!", "What if...?" Since I already felt comfortable with who I am, I had to focus on step #2. I asked myself, "Why am I doing this? What do I want to get out of this, anyway?" The reason quickly came to me. I was helping raise awareness, in a positive way, to help increase the self-esteem of teens and women nationwide. Then I was able to shift out of my fears. I stood up straight, took a deep breath, put a smile on my face, strutted my stuff on that runway...and it was over before I even knew it!

Best of all, none of those fears came true. Overcoming them by just doing it increased my overall confidence by leaps and bounds in all areas of my life. The key to being confident is to believe with all your heart and soul who you are, what you want and then do it! Becoming a confident woman will make you will feel happier, more secure and extra attractive. The greatest reward though is you will soon find everything begins to flow easily and effortlessly into your life.

# Pay It Forward

### Jolynn Van Asten

**Pay it forward is not "scratch my back, I'll scratch yours."**

You enter a networking meeting filled with women excited to share with you all about their businesses. You secure your nametag and quietly head for the restroom to freshen up before you introduce yourself to this cluster of current strangers. As you lean into the mirror to look at your luscious lipstick, a woman in a dark blue business suit exits the stall behind you. "Suzanne, is that you?"

"Yes, yes it is me"—you smile and are concerned that she is going to pitch her business to you right there in the loo.

"Suzanne, I just had a flash of inspiration! I *need* one more gal to be a hostess for me this week. Can you *Pleeezzee* do it? I'll throw a party for you. I promise, it will be the biggest widget party you've ever held!"

Your mind begins to twirl as you think, "Maybe the hostess seeker from the stall was really having just a hot flash, not an inspiration flash...."

Pay it forward, is *not* "scratch my back, I'll scratch yours." As good as a well-performed back scratch may feel, a day of giving just to give feels immeasurably better.

Remember when JFK said, "And so, my fellow Americans, ask not what your country can do for you; ask what you can do for your country." Well, my fellow networking sisters, ask not what your networking group can do for you, ask what you can do for your group.

Now, I am not saying you should not 'get your needs met' or ask for help, or ask for hostesses or for a second helping of pasta primavera. *I am* saying that when our hearts are in the right place, and we are in the right frame of mind, with a proverbial pay it forward attitude, we not only will bless the lives and businesses of others, we will naturally, beyond what we ever could have predicted, bless our own lives and businesses.

When I decided to become a licensee for The Joy of Connecting®, I knew a few women I could invite. I knew I wanted to start this group to grow my own network of fabulous friends and women, and of course grow my http://www.sendbettercards.com business. However, I also knew if I called and said something like the following: "Hi, is this Mary? Great! Mary, I am starting a women's networking group, you know, I am a rep for a greeting card company, and I know you would so love to use my product, heck, you may even want to sell my product...but anyway, it is twenty-five dollars to come, but it is so worth it, and the food is so yummy, and I need at least twenty people there to make it worth my time..." that not only would I scare the day lights out of every one, I would not be paying it forward.

I chose to do the following: "Hi, is Mary available? (*This is she*), Do you have a minute? (*Well yes, depends what this is about....*) Glad you asked! I saw in the paper that you install window treatments, is that right? (*Yes*) Great! There is a new women's networking group meeting, and I was hoping you could come and share with about twenty women business owners a bit about what you do, and bring some brochures and business cards to share. I would love to spotlight you for about three minutes. We are meeting the fourth Tuesday of January—would that date work for you?" (*Let me check, why yes, it does!*) That's wonderful, now, there will be a fabulous dinner that night, and the cost for the event is 25.00. You can register at ___site or send me a check. Which do you prefer?

See the difference? It was all about her, and *I meant it*. People know when you don't really mean what you are saying. Because Mary felt important, and was clear that an opportunity to be spotlighted was present, she came and had a great time, met new contacts, and even gave me a great referral that evening. All in all, stop and think before you speak. Ask yourself: "Is this an appropriate time to request an appointment with this person?" Use your skills to take you to the top, and have people flock to *you* in the loo, instead of running out the door away from *you*.

# 36

# Open Yourself To Possibilities

**Tonya Joy**

**There is an effective connection waiting to be revealed to you too; it is guaranteed.**

Network meetings are all designed to assist business growth because they connect people. It is the effective connections that I build through a network that spreads my brand and increases my business. I have a group of supporters constantly talking about and referencing my services and products. Often, this brand advocacy develops without much effort on my part. However, there is one essential ingredient to my network success formula and that is *me*.

Have you ever had one of these thoughts, "If I attend one more networking meeting, I will scream" or "Oh, I have tried network meetings and they don't work for me?" I certainly have. When I respond to networking with this attitude, I have noticed that my thoughts actually prevent me from getting the results that can skyrocket my business growth. One of the most productive ways that I effectively connect with other people at networking events is to release any negativity, doubt, or preconceived ideas about the event. Once I was asked to attend a networking group by a business contact. I remember thinking, "I don't want to speak about my services to them; I have been to their meeting before without results." Well, I went anyway. As it happened I met a business owner that had a connection to another business that was seeking my services, which resulted in a six-figure income for me. If I had decided to skip the meeting based on my assumption, then I would have missed that effective connection.

As a result, I have learned to be willing to release my assumptions. I open myself to the possibilities that networking events can provide by asking, "Can I *really know* all the contacts and resources that one person can bring to my business if I remain closed to possibilities?"

Recently ABC Primetime conducted The Small World Project to test the social interconnectivity theory: 'six degrees of separation.' Approximately, 60,000 people in 170 countries participated in the project and thousands of connections were made between people. The result was six connections or fewer between any one participant and the person they were assigned to find in the project. When I read this fact, I realized, 'Wow. I really am six people or less from my ideal customer that wants my services, pays me substantially, and remains loyal to my business."

Therefore, my business connections are all around me and here are simple steps that bring me tangible results:

- I decide what type of connection I need. My decision is focused on my current business need: ideal customer or strategic partner. I have found that the key is to be specific about the type of connection my business needs now. My intentions are more powerful with clarity. When I started my business several years ago, I needed customers quickly. I thought my services could assist any person and I would have customers within weeks. However, I found out that my services are really designed for a specific niche. Once I focused on a specific target market or connection, then my income doubled and continues to do so.
- I align my thoughts with that connection. Before I attend a network event, I decide, "I intend to create a successful connection to an ideal customer and I know it will work out." Some time ago, I attended a luncheon and I refined my marketing message to share with that group. However, as the event had presenters, I did not speak. At the end of luncheon, the woman across the table asked me about my business. I explained my business development services to her and she became both a customer and provided referrals that totaled $10K.

My experience has proven that when I release my assumptions and open myself to possibilities then I make effective connections. There is an effective connection waiting to be revealed to you too; it is guaranteed.

# Listen With Your Heart

**Cassandra Wind**

**Heartfelt listening requires you to connect with the other person at an emotional level.**

My instructor from the Midwest College of Oriental Medicine suggested to our class that if we wanted to become great practitioners that we should read 'The Zen of Listening' by Rebecca Z. Shafir. I picked the book up and read about half of it as I finished college back in 2005. The book was insightful and I applied the concepts immediately to my daily routine. Three months later, I graduated and found myself inundated with the tasks of creating a business, marketing, networking, and balancing my life as a single mom.

The next couple of years flew by and business was increasing steadily yet I was frustrated that my income was not covering all my costs and I was no longer enjoying working with my clients. The summer of 2008 I found myself pondering the question once again: Should I get a full-time job? Am I doing the best for my kids? It did not take me long to reflect on the pros and cons of returning to the workplace and to see that I just needed to look at where I was stuck in my beliefs. Suddenly, I thought about what my teacher had said and opened 'The Zen of Listening.' The book fell open to a random page and I read the following sentence:

> "What are the obstacles that keep us from getting the whole message in these should-listen activities, and why can't we let ourselves accept a differing point of view?"

I took the next couple of days to reflect on how I interacted with people I was comfortable with throughout my day. When I found myself uncomfortable interacting with someone, I noted that as well. As I compared these situations and my reactions, I found a great disparity between my thoughts and my heart. I went back and reviewed the book once more and spent time thinking about the clients I was having success with and those I was not. How did I approach each of them?

My first awareness was that I listened to each differently. I noticed that with clients that I felt uncomfortable with I took more of an authoritative approach and asked fewer questions. I found it difficult to listen to them and found myself cutting them off. I was more relaxed with those clients who were progressing and open to my ideas and my healing concepts. I took more time to clarify their needs and address their fears. I became aware that I was focusing more on outcomes, prejudices and agendas with those that really needed me to be hearing them. Again, I remembered these two quotes from the book:

> "Every time we truly listen to people different from ourselves, they give us an opportunity to see a view through another window."
> "Listen first to understand."

As I returned to work the following Monday, I brought this welcome insight and began to implement it with each client. Before I approached anyone, I checked in to see where my thoughts were. Was I in a place to actively listen, to really understand their needs and fears? I observed their body language and listened to the words they used and how they expressed themselves. This helps me identify if the are auditory, visual or kinesthetic learners. Once I have this information, I am ready to respond in a way that the person will feel heard.

I believe that the success of my business and networking comes from my practice of active listening with heart. Active listening requires you to be aware of your thoughts, attitudes and agendas when dealing with others. Heartfelt listening requires you to connect with the other person at an emotional level. Listening with your heart creates understanding and understanding lets another know they have been heard. Being heard is where trust begins and relationships blossom!!!

# 38

## Get Off The Computer, Step Away From The Keyboard

### Meghan Peters

**With emails and text messaging, it is no wonder that human interaction has become more like a science project than an art.**

In today's world, technology seems to be taking over basic communication. With emails and text messaging, it's no wonder that human interaction has become more like a science project than an art. Isn't it just too easy to ignore a conversation when it's on a computer or telephone screen? The delete button sometimes seems to be flashing at me when I'm busy or working on something else that seemed to be more important at that moment.

If it's true that we are becoming more technological, does it also mean that we have to become typewritten words instead of voices? Get off your computer and step away from the keyboard!

I know it's just too easy when we can send out information to the masses with hitting one button versus spending five hours talking repetitively on the telephone. But honestly, if I don't know the email address, how do I know it's safe to open with all of the viruses going around? It's true that cold calling is uncomfortable. It's also true that too many *no, thank you's* (if remembered), are discouraging. Yet, as the second rule of networking says, make every connection count. With Bonnie's permission, let me add to that by saying, "Make every connection personal!"

Pick up the telephone and dial a *number*, do not type a text message. Less than ten years ago we had no problem with picking up the telephone and calling people to invite them to a meeting or a party. Auto-dial and favorites lists have taken the place of remembering a phone number. With a phone call, that invite becomes personal, a personal connection. Who can say no to a live voice without giving a reason for a decline?

Mass communication is often misleading because unless the invitee responds, there's no way to ensure she received and read the invitation. There's no way to ensure she doesn't have any questions. A live voice is readily available to give full details, leaving nothing to the imagination. Without calling one another, there's no way to convey the importance, moreover, the necessity for women to come together to share ideas, offer advice or show support. A little thing like making that personal phone call and extending the invitation personally makes that invite meaningful. It can also make all the difference for a relationship's survival.

I am new to this strange idea of networking, though I have been doing it for years. I hear myself telling more people, "Don't call, I'm better and faster on email." But who doesn't want to hear another person's voice to offer support and love? Too often, things are lost in translation and how better to explain that idea than the computer? A sense of humor does not translate through an email even if you include the smiley face or LOL.

When I held my first Joy of Connecting meeting, I must have dropped off over fifty invitations all around town. If there was a woman's name on the door, I left an invitation. I did not take a single business card and I did not make one follow-up phone call. Out of all of those invitations, not one person came. 'Why,' you ask?

Let me tell you that for my second meeting, I got on the phone and personally called about forty businesswomen I found on the Internet. At that March meeting, twenty-two women were present. At the April meeting, I depended on those participants to bring a friend or spread the word. Though I sent out email invitations, I did not make a single phone call. Ten women were at the meeting in April. Do you see a pattern? The phone is a powerful networking tool; probably the most powerful tool if not meeting face to face. This story proves my theory.

We cannot expect our peers to drop what they are doing to come to our events, offer advice or show support if we can't take the five minutes to make that personal contact. So go ahead, turn off your computer and step away from the keyboard! Pick up the telephone and dial a phone number; let the world hear your beautiful voice! To make every connection count, we need to make it personal!

# 39

## Treat Every "NO" As a "YES"

### Andrea Dudzic-Salter

**You never know who the person you are chatting with may know.**

Pounding the pavement (door-to-door sales) and cold calling can be grueling. Facing an individual or business owner that in your heart you feel your services can truly benefit and fearing that "no" can take the fun out of your job. That is, unless you start telling yourself (and believing it) that every time you hear that "no" you are one step closer to your "yes." Some like to say it's a numbers game. It can be foreseen that way, but to me it's not a game. It's my passion and my livelihood. When I started in the insurance sales industry I was taught to call, call, call, and not stop until I got my "yes." Some days I called ten people or businesses and sometimes it took me 100 calls and ten hang ups before I got through to someone. There were days that I called and was ready to burst into tears but I kept telling myself "I'm one step closer to my "yes" and there it was. It was always one call or appointment away.

Sell yourself! Don't be discouraged if someone doesn't see the benefit of your services the first time you attempt at connecting with them. Take a breath and simply ask when they would be open to discussion. Use open ended questions. Don't allow the individual to be able to answer with a simple "yes" or that dreadful "no." Allow them to think about what they are answering to. Many of my current clients started off as "no's." I asked the questions, I was persistent, and I believed I could help...what's the worst that happen? They could say "no" again...or they could say, "yes."

There are thousands of salespeople out there, but not all of them are persistent and not all know how to take that "no." Set yourself out from the rest. Do your research; know who you are approaching and how your services can benefit them. Then convince yourself of that. If you can't convince yourself, how are you going to convince anyone else? Show your passion and your knowledge.

When you are trying to make that connection at a networking event, ask questions, and learn as much as you can about the individual or business. Take a sincere interest and try to sell yourself quickly and to the point. You may not be able to help that individual at that moment, but he or she may know ten people that may. You never now who the person you are chatting with may know. Look at your "no's" as more possible connections. Ask them *who* they know (not if they know) that would benefit from what you have to offer, and be specific in what you are looking for in a referral. Nine times out of ten they will know at least one person they could connect you with and that person could know ten more connections for you. Remember, those "no's" can turn into your best referral sources. Now it's up to you to follow up, guide, and take care of those referrals and more will follow.

Once I learned that treating every "no" as one step closer to my "yes" I was relieved. I was able to keep a positive attitude towards network-ing and approaching new people. I have been able to grow my business dramatically every year and never pass up a chance to hear another "no," because in my heart I know that each one could very well turn into a "yes."

# 40 Connect With The Magic Of Charisma

### Linda Wind

**An attribute coveted by the masses, pursued by the brave and possessed only by those willing to go the extra mile in its elusive pursuit.**

Charisma...defined as the ability of an individual to influence, charm or inspire large numbers of people. It is an attribute coveted by the masses, pursued by the brave and possessed only by those willing to go the extra mile in its elusive pursuit. It is also defined as an extraordinary power, the ability to perform miracles. It requires an essential understanding of and attention to the ever-changing dynamics of two simple words—people skills. I never cease to be amazed at the ease and grace with which some people conduct their lives, moving so beautifully through the hours and minutes of their many challenges and opportunities, their continual ups and downs, yet all the while striving to overcome those challenges and take advantage of their opportunities, no matter how large or how small, and somehow manage to leave behind a legacy of happiness and love. And as an added bonus, these exceptional people have learned, as part of their life lessons, the uncommon knack of how to make a difference in other people's lives. How do they do it and what can we learn from them? I, for one, am convinced that this magical attribute is nothing more than a significant recipe comprised of equal parts of these prized ingredients: *caring about others, giving back, and creating charismatic connections.*

The first two are self-explanatory; they come truly from the heart and are inherent to someone's unique personality and physical and mental chemistry. Creating charismatic connections, however, is more about a direct choice of action than an innate feeling, and for sure is the pathway to developing deep personal satisfaction and unprecedented success in life. We all have our unique capabilities and talents, and I feel that my special legacy is one of connecting profoundly with others, personally and professionally, and in turn partnering with other people so that their lives might benefit from that mutual relationship in some way. Let me explain.

Ever since I was a little girl it was important for me to create connections with others and surround myself with other girls my age who got along well and were compatible. As I grew older and entered the business world, I intuitively connected with my clients very deeply. Sure, I wanted them to be happy and well taken care of—the 'under-promise and over-deliver' mantra—but it was more than that. I wanted to develop meaningful, long-lasting relationships with them. I found out, for example, when their birthdays were, who their family members were (and their names and their pets names).... I was very clear from the get-go that what I really wanted was a long term relationship with them that would create a win-win for both of us, and I told them so! I became very successful in my career and ultimately ended my 20-year corporate stint as the top female executive in a Fortune 500 company. But please know that my driving motivation was first and foremost making sure they were taken care of, and not by the subsequent success that would most assuredly follow.

When I made the transition from 'corporate tour to entrepreneur' my action plan was the same—to create caring, meaningful connections that would make a difference, and the past twelve years have been woven throughout with the platinum threads of positive relationships that I have been fortunate enough to realize. And I continue to do this every day in every relationship that I manifest. What originally started as Possible Woman Enterprises in 1997 is now Wind Enterprises Inc., and this entity has set the stage for what now has become my life mission: Making a unique and significant difference in the lives of women globally. And I have accomplished this, and continue to accomplish this in many ways, mostly through the magic of charisma that is now so much a part of who I am. It also manifests itself through the acknowledgment of the fact that we are more...more than our name alone, more than all that we may own...more than what our parents bred, more than what our teachers said. And I have learned much in this lifetime, and will continue to learn, to grow, to achieve, to care, to love deeply, to reach for the stars with every breath I take. This is my truth; my magic, my charisma, my legacy for all eternity.

# Develop a Social Media Mindset

**Tiffany Odutoye**

**The idea behind social media is to get into real-time conversation with your market.**

Remember the first time you went to the dentist and heard the whirr and buzz of the drill? It made your skin crawl, didn't it? If you're like most people, to this day every time you hear that sound, your skin crawls and you get a particular jarring sensation in the jaw, even if you're not the one getting the treatment.

When old-school marketing experts hear about social media marketing, something similar happens to them. The term 'marketing' sends them into the selling mode straightaway. And that's where they make their first, and biggest, mistake. Traditional marketing strategies center on the motto 'build and business will boom.' The marketing medium is used for a one-sided broadcast of the marketing message. There are no overt attempts to build a community or nurture the brand value of a product.

Social media is a different tool altogether. To use it in the framework of old marketing ideas is missing the point. True, vast opportunities do exist, and these lucky breaks can be leveraged, but marketers need to develop a particular mindset to get the most from social media.

The idea behind social media is to get into real-time conversation with your market. This marketing medium must be participatory for it to succeed.

So, how can you make your social media atmosphere the kind of place where everyone drops by for a visit?

Think about this for a moment: We may or may not listen to people we know, but we definitely pay attention to people we like. So, how can you make the important transition from 'know' to 'like' through social media?

- Establish your presence: Dive right in and set the conversational ball rolling.
- Listen: People will talk about you and your brand, whether you like it or not. This is a first-rate feedback loop you're in. So, listen carefully.
- Give: Ever noticed how a spade is always taking whatever you dig toward it? Chuck this mentality. Instead of taking all the while, be a giver, and give without any expectation of returns. Give more entertainment, information, discounts and satisfaction. Become a rich resource center.
- Expand: Meet, connect and develop your pool of contacts.
- Learn: Be the best in your niche.
- Collaborate: Do not isolate your competition. Engage them.

With these thoughts in your mind, you're ready to start networking for business.

If you want to become the societal hub, the 'pull force' that attracts customers to your company, there are certain ground rules to follow. The first is to be aware of the social media etiquette.

*Just because there's no one there but you and your monitor, don't think that social media is like the wild, wild West! You can't draw your guns and go bang, bang. If you want to be popular, you must play nice in the sandbox.*

Here's how:

**Avoid the keyboard gangsta syndrome.** Never say online, what you wouldn't in real life.

**Give more than you receive.** 80/20 rule.

**Mind what you say.** Never say in a comment what has the potential to be viewed as "nasty."

**Don't pitch.** Do not turn your profile into a sales pitch to harvest more contacts. Social networking is about connecting with people.

**Give quality content.** People will come to you if your content is good enough to stand on its own. Oh, and while we're at it, let's get something else straight: Don't 'airlift' content from other websites.

# 42

# These Are Our Rules. What Are Yours?

## Bonnie Ross-Parker and Cindy Elsberry

**You, no doubt, have your own behaviors and ideas of how being an effective connector works for you.**

When Cindy and I decided to collaborate on this project, we had no idea who would write what, what kind of response we'd receive and if we'd get enough 'submissions' to make this 42 Rules publication a viable resource for the reader. We faced a blank sheet of paper, not sure how we would ever pull this off, who to ask and if we could really pull this off! To our delight and amazement, we did pull it off. We are thrilled with the results. By assembling great minds with great ideas/strategies, this book has surpassed all expectations. Our contributors selflessly offered their expertise on what makes connection work for them and provided insights we could not have done on our own. As with any labor of love, we combined time and talent to make this a stand out, one of a kind resource. We hope you agree and will not only read the rules in any order of your choosing, but also choose to implement them in your daily life.

Of course, we hope the journey doesn't stop here. You, no doubt, have your own behaviors and ideas of how being an effective connector works for you. Those we've shared are only a sampling of what is possible. After all, connecting is the center of all of our lives. No one chooses to journey alone. Life is meant to be shared. Joy is in the shared journey. It's those opportunities we say "yes" to the people we meet or invite along the way, and the "ah ha" moments that awaken us to a new way of looking at something familiar. Our journeys continue day to day, as one experience follows another. The journey embraces people who impact us, circumstances and changes we can't control, the choices and decisions we make and the effect of those actions over time. How we conduct ourselves and the value we place on our relationships determine the quality of our life. What rules/ideas/strategies you choose to implement—ours and yours—will serve as the platform from which you create meaningful and effective connections.

The majority of the contributing writers for '42 Rules for Effective Connections' are part of a national organization called The Joy of Connecting®. It's a non-membership, national community of women who meet monthly to share resources, expand and strengthen relationships and foster business for themselves and for others. Their rules are the basis of this book. Writing a book together has solidified our community and enriched our lives beyond the words conveyed. I hope you, too, will choose to consider being an author or collaborating with others to share your ideas with those who will be eager to learn from you as well. Both Cindy and I would welcome hearing from you, our readers. Please consider dropping us a line on how one or more of our rules has impacted your life or a rule you'd like to offer that we could share with others. You may contact Cindy at CindyElsberry@gmail.com and Bonnie at Bootgirl@TheJOYofConnecting.com.

Consider registering for our gift to you at http://www.TheJOYofConnecting.com—an e-book called: 'Y.O.U.: Set a High Standard for Being Human.'

# Resources

## Web Resources:

Bonnie Ross-Parker
(http://www.BonnieRossParker.com) - Bonnie,
a.k.a. America's Connection Diva, is an author
and speaker who focuses on networking through
her publications, workshops and keynote pre-
sentations.

Bumble Bee Virtual Assistant Services
(http://tinyurl.com/llhego) - An affordable way to
lighten your workload while you focus on building
your business.

The Direct Selling Women's Alliance
(http://www.mydswa.org) - You're invited to
become a part of a community that offers encouragement, education and ideas for growing your
network marketing or party plan business.

Idea Marketers (http://www.IdeaMarketers.com)
- Your online publicity hub and a great resource
center.

The Joy of Connecting®
(http://www.TheJOYofConnecting.com) - An innovative customer acquisition/marketing
program for women who are serious about
growing their business.

The Network Marketing Magazine
(http://tinyurl.com/lje4my) - The #1 source for
anyone in the network marketing profession.

Wind Enterprises, Inc. (http://www.WindEnterprises.com) - Founded in 1996, Wind Enterprises, Inc., is a corporation committed to the personal and professional development of the female business executive and career woman.

## Book Resources:

'Walk In My Boots—The Joy of Connecting' by Bonnie Ross-Parker - Journey with Bonnie as she shares how connections enrich our lives and the lives of those who journey with us.

'Y.O.U.: Set A High Standard for Being Human' by Bonnie Ross-Parker - 15 key strategies on how you can do a better job in your personal and professional relationships.

Order Bonnie's books at http://www.bonnierossparker.com.

# B Contributors' Background

**Anne Alberg (Rule 12)**, Global Networking Diva, is known for her vast network of who is doing what. She contributes her success as a professional networker to the fact that she truly loves people and enjoys finding out who they are and what they are looking for personally or professionally. Anne has a passion for helping others acquire the skills necessary to live their best life, including teaching them to be in contribution to others. Professionally, Anne is dedicated to inspiring busy professionals to make better choices towards a healthy lifestyle and to have fun! Through extensive research regarding toxicity in America and nutritional deficiency in today's food choices; and her own personal experience with toxic methane gas exposure, Anne is driven to share her message. Adopting a nutritional, cleansing lifestyle is an effective technique to optimize your health, rejuvenate your body, regain clarity of mind, and help you to safely and easily lose weight.

Anne graduated from the University of Washington with a degree in marketing and entrepreneurship. She has developed a diverse business background working for a variety of start-up companies, including extensive international travel. Anne has been an active board member of various business organizations since 1989, such as the Medical Marketing Association, Business and Professional Women, Women's Advisory Council for the National Association for the Self Employed, and she served as Managing Director for eWomenNetwork. Anne currently serves on the Puget Sound Business Journal's Women's Advisory Council and is a Co-Founder of Woodinville Women and Wine. Today you can find Anne networking on various online social networks.

Anne Alberg
Email: diva@annealberg.com
Website: http://www.annealberg.com

**Debbie Baus (Rule 15)** is an online business professional specializing in helping businesses build profitable relationships. Coming from a technical background as a cryptologic officer in the U. S. Navy and a software management professional, Debbie naturally gravitated to the Internet and launched her own web development and Internet consulting company. In the process of searching out new and unique tools to help her clients build their businesses, she discovered Send Out Cards, a unique and powerful relationship marketing tool that enables businesses to reach out and touch their client base regularly while saving time and money. To see if your business could be building more profitable relationships, contact her by email or learn more about her relationship marketing on her website.

Debbie Baus
Email: CardsAlive@gmail.com
Website: http://MyCardStories.com

**Caroline Scranton Bell (Rule 25)** is an award-winning executive with over eighteen years of Marketing and Executive Sales experience across all segments of the hospitality and food service industries. She has taken the experience she gained while with corporate giants Diners Club and American Express and coupled that with her extensive personal experience in senior planning and care to develop her new company.

As the founder of her practice, **Preparing for Care, LLC,** Caroline uses the hands-on experience she has gained with her 87-year-old father to provide much needed education, support and guidance to adult children who are about to or are now caring for their senior parents. Preparing for Care, LLC, is an information portal, helping people learn how to keep their parents independent but connected, choose a place for their parents plus much more. It is a resource center —for those needing to find reliable, vetted specialized services for their parents. But most of all, it is a safe haven for one of the most trying and emotionally charged situations anyone can face—one for which most of us are simply not prepared. Preparing for Care helps others through this frightening ordeal or helps them prepare prior to it, with high-class, top-notch, caring, empathetic friends on their side (and on their parents' side) in and before the time of need.

Caroline Scranton Bell
Phone: 770-377-9409
Email: Caroline@preparingforcare.com
Website: http://www.preparingforcare.com

**Cindy Borassi (Rule 3)** is the mama of two creative, loving and energy-filed children—Isabella and Christopher, and is married to her friend and biggest supporter Charles. She is also the founder of the Growinglove.net website and 'Seeds of Love'—a *free* bi-weekly E-Zine for modern yogis and yoginis who want to create an authentic and spirit-filled life for their families. Previously, Cindy enjoyed 15 years developing and managing international consulting projects for non-profit, government and for-profit organizations including the U.S. Department of Defense, the U.S. Agency for International Development and corporations such as Gillette and Xerox. As an expert in business development, project management and fundraising she conceptualized and managed innovative and multi-tiered projects throughout Russia, Central Asia, Ukraine, Egypt, Africa, Latin America and the United States. Early in her career she realized the importance of personal connections and networking in building effective, long-term and personal relationships with her clients and staff. Cindy has been consistently recognized for her achievements in managing capital, people, strategies and performance.

In 1998 Cindy was introduced to the ancient practice of yoga and shortly thereafter became a certified 200-hour RYT in AtmaYoga and a certified YogaFit Perinatal Instructor. She has been teaching yoga since 1990 and currently teaches prenatal, adult, baby and mommy (or daddy), and children's yoga classes. Cindy's mission is to inspire others to Be and Become their birthright of perfection through the practice of Yoga—Breath Work and Meditation—inspiring, safe, and supportive classes, wellness retreats and workshops. Recognizing the need for events and workshops focused on nurturing and supporting the women in her community, Cindy joined the growing network of The Joy of Connecting® licensees. Cindy looks forward to creating unique and inspiring events for the women and families in her community.

Cindy Borassi
Founder - GrowingLove.net
Phone: 914-400-6675
Email: cindy@growinglove.net
Website: http://www.GrowingLove.net

**Susan Brown, Ed. S, (Rule 7)** a certified coach, consultant and founder of *Impact Coaching* works with highly motivated individuals to create high performance work environments where professional and personal excellence are the norm. She helps others discover their full potential and equips them with skills to more impactfully develop others. As a former teacher, school administrator and an 11-year breast cancer thriver, Susan combines all of her life's experiences and passions to coach and train current and rising leaders. Her philosophy is that each of us is called to be a leader at some time, in some form, that is unique to our talents and passions. In addition to being a certified Emotional Intelligence coach, Susan is a certified Live A New Life Story™ trainer. She is a frequent guest on radio shows and has given numerous interviews, workshops and classes addressing such issues as using the power of story as a catalyst for change and leveraging emotional intelligence to create success. For additional information about her classes, coaching and consulting, visit Susan's website.

Susan presents at local and national conferences, delivers keynote addresses and facilitates retreats. Some of her recent topics include:

- Happiness Is A Choice
- Energy Boosters: Fuelers or Foolers
- Live a New Leadership Life Story
- Creating the Joyful Spirit
- Emotional Intelligence: A Key to Success in Work and Life

Susan Brown
Phone: 678-787-2406
Email: susan@impactcoaching-empower.com
Website: http://www.impactcoaching-empower.com

**Andrea Brunache (Rule 28)** is a nationally known and well respected business owner in Metro Atlanta. Andrea has set the bar high for women-owned business and is helping others succeed in business development, health awareness and spiritual growth. Andrea is a Health and Wellness representative with *Arbonne International* which promotes "Thinking Green" by using safe, all-natural, plant-based botanical products that deliver beneficial results from the inside and out for everyone. To show support for various health awareness initiatives, Andrea is a member and marathon runner for the Joints in Motion Arthritis Foundation and the Susan G. Komen Breast Cancer Foundation. Andrea is strongly committed to helping other business owners prosper and grow their businesses.

A Licensee with the The Joy of Connecting®, Andrea facilitates a relaxed networking dinner for professional women-owned businesses in the *Buford*, GA, area. Andrea's professional work experience and achievements span back to her home state—The Big Apple, New York, where she worked fifteen years in Legal/Administration and Labor/Employment Law and has been instrumental in her husband's Government Construction and Janitorial business. Andrea holds high standards of excellence which she brilliantly demonstrates by organizing, participating and facilitating Trade shows, Expos and Fundraisers throughout Atlanta. Andrea resides with her husband and three children in North Atlanta, GA. She is a proud member of Sufficient Grace Tabernacle in Lilburn, GA. Thinking Green and Enjoying Connecting, Andrea is a conscientious, woman-owned business professional who takes prides in her work in making a difference in the lives of others.

Andrea Brunache/CEO and Founder
Phone: 678-768-6481
Email: abrunache10@yahoo.com
Website: http://www.growinggreenexpo06182009.eventbrite.com

**Antoinette Corbin (Rule 6)** was born and raised in the small community of Swiftwater, in the Mississippi Delta. Her love for the arts began in elementary school, where she acted in several class and school plays. She began writing during her sophomore year in high school, with a creative writing assignment. Poetry and short stories followed, and during this same time, she began working on a book project.

Her pursuit of the arts continued through college, where she majored in Speech Communications. She was a member of the drama team, starring in the final semester production; a member of the forensics team, placing in numerous speech tournaments; and a contributor for the university newspaper. Antoinette has since written poetry for friends and family for special occasions, including the weddings of a friend's daughter and her pastor's daughter.

Antoinette currently resides in the Mississippi Delta with her husband and two children, where she is preparing to launch her own desktop publishing business. Her poetry and other written works, as well as other information about her, can be found on her websites.

Antoinette Corbin
Emails: annchenette@hotmail.com (primary)
       mrscorbin_0516@yahoo.com (alternate)
Websites: http://givinittoyastraight.blogspot.com/
       http://fromawriterspov.ning.com/profile/AntoinetteCorbin
(Poetry can be found under the tab 'Open Poetry Café.')

**Heather Doering (Rule 21)** is a Team Leader with SimplyFun, an innovative company whose mission is to help America rediscover how to play. Heather loves being full-time CEO of her own business, which is secondary to being a full-time wife and mother. Being her own boss enables Heather to set her own schedule and work around the many volunteer activities, sports practices, and family commitments while still running a successful business. Goal setting has enabled Heather to earn two SimplyFun incentive trips in less than two years, has propelled her into leadership, and has earned her numerous awards. *You* have the power to succeed—set your goals, then achieve them. *You* control your destiny!

Heather Doering
Phone: 734-414-0534
Website: http://heatherdoering.simplyfun.com

**Andrea Dudzic-Salter (Rule 39)** was born in Milwaukee, WI, and now resides just outside the city in Greenfield where she brokers health and life insurance (http://www.etruehealth.com) and is a licensee for The Joy of Connecting®. Andrea has worked in the service industry since she was 14 years old and has excelled in promotions and management throughout the years. In 2004, she and her husband had their first child and decided that 70-hour work weeks, nights and weekends were not going to work. Andrea decided to venture out and work for herself; she went back to school and became licensed to sell insurance. She has since had a 2nd child and continues to put her energy in the success of her business (and in being a great mom). She has taken part in numerous sales and marketing trainings and continues with her studies today. Andrea has taken a great interest in marketing with other businesswomen. She opens her home monthly to women in Wisconsin to showcase their business in front of 15 to 30 other women. She tries to create or find new ways to be an effective saleswoman on a continuous basis. Andrea sees *every* situation as an opportunity for growth; if not for her business, for someone else's business, or even for her personal life.

Andrea Salter
Email: andreasalter@tds.net
Website: http://www.etruehealth.com

**Lyn-Dee Eldridge (Rule 29)** is a Motivational Speaker/Coach/ Published Author who has touched thousands of lives! Achievements and accomplishments that most only dream about when being "The Obvious Expert in Sales and Building Relationships!"

**In Lyn-Dee's own words…**

My mission has always been to "pay it forward" by helping as many people as I can, find the greatness within themselves. We live in a world that is sometimes not so colorful, not so fair and sometimes what we think to be a dead-end street. Everyone has the right to live; no one should feel as if they are a failure or be told what they not capable of doing. Everyone has the right to create a lifestyle that they dream about. My diverse background has given me the experience to help others overcome adversity and have triumphant success. It's our full life experiences that make us who we are today. So because of the good fortunes I've experienced in the game of life, I've gone from the very bottom to the top! The one thing that has always been consistent was empowering others to do what I have already accomplished and helping thousands around the world to become all they can be! Helping others achieve the greatness within them is the most exciting, fulfilling and rewarding experience I have ever had and I look forward to many, many years of helping others like you create the greatness within! I can't wait to meet you in person and share a smile!

Lyn-Dee Eldridge
Email: info@lyn-dee.com
Website: http://www.Lyn-Dee.com

**R. Jill Fink (Rule 4)** is an author and artist, and President of The Purple Monkey Soap Company. As a child, her skin would peel off of her hands, and rashes and red blotches appeared after every bath. Jill's parents were told that she had a hereditary skin condition that would cause lifelong suffering. Jill began studying aromatherapy in 1993 while part of a management team at a health food store. She graduated from massage school and passed the Florida State Boards, becoming a licensed Massage Therapist in 1998. Her studies also included healing arts such as Reflexology, Shiatsu and Reiki. Due to Jill's lifelong battle with allergies to soaps, lotions, fabric softeners, and other cosmetics, she later left her career in massage but kept helping others through aromatherapy.

During the summer of 2006, Jill's skin condition was greatly exacerbated. Out of desperation, she decided to make her own old-fashioned soap from botanical oils and lye (sodium hydroxide) just like her maternal grandmother had done. After the required three-week cure time, Jill used her handmade soap and her suffering ceased. Realizing that her skin condition was due to the harsh chemicals contained in store-bought brands instead of hereditary allergies, Jill ecstatically started creating more all-natural products for herself, her friends and her family. Her passion grew into a business and The Purple Monkey Soap Company was born. Purple Monkey now produces over 40 eco-friendly home, body and pet products without the use of sulphates, glycols, or parabens. None of the raw materials used nor the finished products are ever tested on animals. The Purple Monkey Soap Company's mission is to provide quality products, exemplary customer service and education.

R. Jill Fink
Email: pmsoapco@aol.com
Website: http://www.purplemonkeysoapcompany.com

**Lori Finlay-Hamilton (Rule 20)** is exuberant about life and brings vitality and passion to everything she does. She has a sense of wonder and strong desire to impact others that developed in her early years. She loves working with smart, gutsy, and innovative people. Lori's successful career in nursing was a platform for her to not only impact others, but also demonstrate her desire for excellence and leadership. After years at the bedside, she became a nurse practitioner, and clinical faculty member at the University of Utah College of Nursing. She has also been a sought-after trainer all over the world though her nursing career and her own business, Women, Wisdom and Wellness, Inc. She was awarded the "Who's Who for Integrative Health and Wellness Education."

Her entrepreneurial career of 14 years combined with her understanding of gender differences has allowed Lori to create powerful partnerships with men and women—on her team, and as a valued member of international advisory boards. Her specialty in Wellness and Complementary/Integrative Medicine motivated her desire to not only understan—but hold safe—the sacred differences between men and women. Honoring the complementary differences of men and women not only creates greater success, but less stress and greater vitality—both personally and professionally. Lori inspires others to excellence. She challenges each to bring their unique vision into reality and creates the freedom for them to soar. Lori's passion is to empower people around the globe to create more than lives of success—success while preserving their vitality and success with significance!

Lori Finlay Hamilton, M.S., APRN, C.S.
Nurse Practitioner, Trainer, Entrepreneur
Phone: 770-449-6499
Email: Lori@LoriFinlayHamilton.com
Website: http://www.LoriFinlayHamilton.com
Visit My Blog: http://InsiderSecretsToWomensVitality.com

**Kathy Greider (Rule 16)** is the founder of *GreiderBiz—Your Business-BOOSTER*. She has been helping people increase efficiency and improve their financial status all her life. Today, she works with small (mostly) women-owned businesses to give a *Boost* to their Bottom Line—something much needed and appreciated in this economy. She loves to network and that is how she meets most of her clients. Kathy is a great connector—probably why she loves being a licensee for The Joy of Connecting®. Kathy enjoys helping business owners. She knows small businesses have the same problems as big businesses—they just don't' have access to the same high-powered resources to deal with their problems. Compliance with ever-changing laws, marketing, web presence, promotions, and networking expertise are ways Kathy help her clients. Kathy works with her clients to discover what they need to *increase their bottom line!*

One client put it this way—"When I worked with Kathy she helped me find the best way to market my business. I thought I knew what I needed, but after talking with Kathy she showed me how one of her *less expensive products*—would work much better for me. She was right—it worked! I've never worked with anyone who *down sells*, but Kathy wants you to use what will work best for your business. *She Listens and She Cares!*" Kathy works with high quality national partners who provide rewards/incentives and expert advice/guidance for small businesses. Follow Kathy on Twitter and checkout her on LinkedIn. Google Kathy Greider, read all about GreiderBiz—Your BusinessBOOSTER. When not working, she enjoys the B's in life—Beaches, Birding, Brewpubs, Being a Babyboomer and her grandson!

Kathy Greider
Phone: 404.313.8208
Email: greiderbiz@yahoo.com
Website: http://www.greiderbiz.com

**Nancy Hayssen (Rule 34)** is a plus size model and author who has been inspiring millions of women worldwide in the body acceptance movement, defying Hollywood standards and setting a new ideal. "You Can Be Sexy at Any Size!" was recently featured on CBS Entertainment Tonight, Fox News and major media promoting the message that in a world of "skinny ideals" over 70% of Americans wear a size 14 or higher. Discover how to increase your own confidence by dressing right for your body type.

Nancy Hayssen
Email: nancy@looksexynow.com
Website: http://www.looksexynow.com

**Susan Hendrix (Rule 13)** after college, worked as a high school math teacher for several years. When her kids were little she wanted to work but also be a 'stay-at-home' mom. She was very fortunate to find a company called Discovery Toys over 20 years ago. It has been exciting to be in a business that rewards Susan for building a team of other like-minded women who want the best for their families and enjoy helping others. She still 'plays for a living,' works flexible hours and loves it!

Susan markets a unique line of safe, fun, educational toys to parents and schools and provides a flexible income opportunity for woman. Discovery Toys are marketed through home parties, fundraisers at schools and organizations and through the website. Susan was recognized with an Innovation Award for Discovery Toys, for the gift baskets that she personalizes and ships nationwide. But her greatest reward has been not only to help children reach their full potential, but to watch women grow and succeed in their own businesses. She is a 'toy lady' for life!

Susan Hendrix
Sales Director
Phone: 404-394-6367
Email: sshebdrix@aol.com
Website: http://www.thetoylady.biz

**Marcie Hooks (Rule 10)** Since retiring from a corporate job, Marcie Hooks became an entrepreneur as an independent distributor with the Shaklee Corporation, the #1 Nutrition Company in the United States. Last year, during the company's global conference, she was honored as a "Star Achiever." She loves sharing and is currently mentoring several people to help them achieve the same success.

There are great nutrition products for the entire family—Children's/Women's/Men's Health; Shaklee Food Supplements and Herbal Products; Non-Toxic *Green* Home cleaning products that work and are economical; Anti-Aging Liquid Dietary Supplement, Air and Water Purification Products, and Stress solutions products. Shaklee also offers a weight management program to help you lose those unwanted pounds and inches. In ten weeks Marcie lost 13 pounds and 14 inches! She began taking Vivix, which was introduced in August and later she visited the office she worked in and one girl squealed at her, "Marcie, you look 25 years younger." The latest products are for babies and kids called ShakleeBaby and ShakleeKids. She also helps people set up a home-based office to earn extra income. You may visit her website to read all about these products.

Marcie Hooks
Email: mhooks1@comcast.net
Website:http://www.shaklee.net/marciehooks

**Tonya Joy (Rule 36)** is founder of Life Balance Strategies, LLC. In 2006, she finally left the corporate world to begin building her own business based on her life purpose and passions. She is a strategic collaborator and development coach for female entrepreneurs. She assists service-based solo entrepreneurs with getting focused on their success and marketing. Her simple, effective strategies assist them with achieving results by moving out of overwhelm and into clarity. She is a dynamic motivational speaker. Claim your free copy of the "End Business Overwhelm in 5 Simple Steps and Achieve Results Immediately" by visiting her website.

Tonya Joy
Email: info@mylifebalancestrategies.com
Website: http://www.mylifebalancestrategies.com

**Dr. Linda Katz (Rule 19)** began her career as an emergency room nurse in Manhattan. Traditional medicine was unable to help her with the pain of migraine headaches, at which time she sought the help of a chiropractor and received amazing results. After completing her studies at Life Chiropractic in Georgia, Dr. Katz opened Fayette Chiropractic Center (FCC) in Fayetteville, Georgia, in 1984. She states, "everyday is a pleasure because I work with a wonderful community that appreciates the benefits of natural health care." She is also a chiropractic orthopedist and has completed an eight-year study in chiropractic pediatrics. She is a member of the Georgia Chiropractic Association, the American Chiropractic Association and the International Pediatric Chiropractic Association.

Today FCC serves the community in helping people with herniated discs avoid surgery by using the VAX-D machine for spinal decompression. FCC staff educates patients with nutritional counseling; detoxification with Isagenix; hydration and keeping the body in the alkaline state to prevent disease with Kangen Water from Enagic, and posture correction with body magic—a custom-fitting garment made by Ardyss. Dr. Katz mentors students of chiropractic in her office and has extended her passion of helping others achieve success to women in Atlanta through The Joy of Connecting®. "Each month I have the pleasure of meeting new women and sharing ideas and techniques to empower us in the business world," she says. Her personal life is rich and challenging. "Emily, my special needs daughter, has opened up a whole new world in treatments. I can now connect, learn and share with other parents customized treatments to maximize the potential of each child. My other daughter, Erin, is an everyday miracle. I get to relive my childhood through her eyes and experience life in a new way."

Dr. Linda Katz
Email: fayettechiro@mindspring.com
Websites: http://www.thejoyofconnecting.com
　　　　　http://www.getwellstat.info
　　　　　http://www.770backpain.com
　　　　　http://www.ardysslife.com

**Wendy Keahi Kirley (Rule 24)** resides on the island of Oahu in Hawaii. A former model, commercial actress, professional pianist and cultural performer, she is also an entrepreneur who has had her own businesses since her teen years, when she began teaching piano. Besides owning a music studio, she's owned a childcare business, an automotive/vehicle transport business, and most recently started a business named after her, KEAHInnovation. A small business professional and a do-it-herselfer, Wendy believes in knowing every aspect of her business and in being capable of doing every part of it herself. Her newest endeavor with KEAHInnovation focuses on helping businesses and individuals thrive through organization, personal development, training and coaching, and a unique style of networking with The Joy of Connecting®. About The Joy of Connecting® in Hawaii, Wendy says, "I'm eager to gather women together for more than food...I want to achieve something for and with them that will make our experience together not only pleasurable, but also profitable!"

When asked about her Hawaiian name, Keahi, that is part of her business name, she explains, "Keahi means 'the fire' and it perfectly describes who I am: I thrive when I am involved in something where I am needed (the fuel to the flame); I stand for what I believe to be right (burn strong); I help others find *their* better way toward achieving their dreams and realizing their life's purpose (light), and I care and share openly and often (warmth)." Wendy's philosophy is evident in KEAHInnovation's motto: *On Fire Creating Success*. She is definitely on fire about all of her involvements pursuant to, not just her own, but to the success of all she encounters through her work.

Wendy Keahi Kirley
Email: keahikirley@hawaiiantel.net
Website: http://KEAHInnovation.wordpress.com

**Michelle Martin (Rule 33)** is the owner/publisher of 'Metro Woman,' a women's guide to businesses in Fort Worth and the surrounding areas. She is committed to supporting local businesswomen through The Joy of Connecting® networking events, and by offering affordable marketing and advertising opportunities through 'Metro Woman.' She resides in Arlington, TX, with her husband and two children. Michelle enjoys volunteering, spending quality time with her family, and mentoring women business owners to create and sustain successful businesses. For more information about Michelle, 'Metro Woman' and Arlington, Texas, The Joy of Connecting® events,

Michelle Martin
Email: fwmetrowoman@sbcglobal.net
Website: http://www.MetroWomanFortWorth.com

**Debbi McCloud, (Rule 31)** is The Joy of Connecting® Licensee for the Locust Grove/McDonough/Stockbridge/Henry County, GA area. When she's not helping others work through IT processes, systems and interpreting techno-jargon, you will find this savvy IT Consultant, who has a desire for everyone to experience love, peace and happiness, checking out the latest in sports and automotives with a particular love for being a part of the action at auto shows, sporting events and browsing car dealerships for their latest line-up.

With a breath of experience in both IT and academia, Debbi McCloud is your "IT-Gal" with a knack for meshing well in groups and easily interacting with people. As co-owner, along with her husband, of DPM Business Solutions, LLC, Debbi provides professional billing and automated cash-flow management services to medical providers and general business owners.

As an only child who comes from a close-knit family, Debbi has a natural gravitation towards people; she's never met a stranger. Debbi's ability to put people at ease and help them make sense of new concepts and processes has won her numerous accolades from her students in her role as Adjunct Instructor at The University of Phoenix and DeVry. "Teaching is rewarding for me. I was inspired to teach because of my early experience as a help desk analyst when I was responsible for solving systems issues through troubleshooting. It gave me great pleasure to help people solve things that make their lives run smoother." She's also had her 15 minutes of fame by landing in Essence Magazine's *Side Hustle* column in the March 2008 edition in which she raved about her love for fashion, jewelry and all things shopping expressed through her hobby as a Fashion Coordinator for the now defunct fashion company, Weekenders.

Debbie McCloud
Website: http://www.dpmbizsolutions.com

**Carolyn B. McCollum (Rule 26)** a native of Cleveland, Ohio, graduated from Elmhurst College in Illinois and Boston University Law School in Massachusetts. While in law school, Carolyn became a flight attendant for Trans World Airlines (TWA), as a summer job. She continued her career as a flight attendant for over 30 years while also pursuing her career as an attorney. During this time Carolyn also became an independent beauty consultant with Mary Kay Cosmetics, Inc.

Carolyn has worked as an attorney in a variety of areas including private practice with her father, Rathuel L. McCollum, in Cleveland, Ohio; the National Labor Relations Board (NLRB) for 19 years as a law clerk to two administrative law judges and as a staff attorney in the Office of the General Counsel. Carolyn also served as the Associate General Counsel for the Epilepsy Foundation of America (EFA). Carolyn is currently an Independent Beauty Consultant with Mary Kay with a goal to become a Mary Kay National Sales Director and to open her own law practice in the near future. Her passions include empowering people, swimming, world travel and staying fit and healthy.

Carolyn is the host of Joy of Connecting in the Washington, DC, metropolitan area.

Carolyn B. McCollum
Email: personal@carolynbmccollum.com
Website: http://www.MaryKay.com/cmccollum

**Carole McNichol (Rule 22)** was born and raised in London, England, to Jamaican immigrants, and then immigrated to the USA in 1977. She was fortunate to be able to work full time and pursue an undergraduate degree. In 1987 Carole graduated from Sacred Heart University in Fairfield, Connecticut, where she received a BS in Finance. At that time she entered the financial services industry, and married the love of her life, mothering his seven children. In 1989, their son was born.

Carole's career started with MetLife, specializing in life insurance products. In 1990 she started a rewarding career with Valic as a Retirement Specialist. After 17 years, Carole felt it was time to launch out on her own so, in 2007, she took the giant leap and became an Independent Advisor with ING Financial Partners to better serve her clients with more personalized services. Carole offers all investment products including health, life and variable annuity products. Over the years she has focused on educating women, with financial workshops and seminars. Carole supports the financial services industry through her membership with Women in Insurance and Financial Services (WIFCS).

Carole presently resides in Georgia with her husband, where they are active members of their church.

Carole McNichol
Investment Adviser Representative
ING Financial Partners
Phone: 678-641-1137
Email: carole.mcnichol@ingfp.com

**Patricia McTier (Rule 30)** graduated from Kennesaw State University where she studied Business Management, Finance, and held the Finance Chair for the Kennesaw Marketing Association. Entering the financial industry shortly after the devastation of September 11, 2001, taught her how to be a resourceful, perseverant and successful asset to both the banks she worked for and her clients. Patti takes pride in the education of her personal and business clients, and stresses the importance of how powerful financial education is, especially during critical times in the economy. In her career as a banker, she has provided advice to regional presidents concerning strategic product placement for National Bank of Commerce, as well as strengthening the new hire process and contributing to the mentoring manual for the Georgia region of RBC Bank. In the future, Patti hopes to bring more financial awareness to the public school curriculum through the education of young people, helping them to become fiscally competent and empowering the community. Patti is a member of: Cumming-Forsyth County Chamber of Commerce, KSU Alumni, Joy of Connecting-Cumming Georgia, Supports Garden of Empowerment, founded by Susan Wilson, Habitat for Humanity, March of Dimes, United Way, and a card carrying member of the Humane Society.

Patricia McTier
Email: pattimctier@gmail.com

**Nancy Munn (Rule 32)** is a true "Jersey Girl;" born and raised in southern New Jersey and now residing in Central Jersey. The first time she moved out of New Jersey was to attend the University of Kentucky. Nancy achieved her B.S. degree in nutrition and food science with a minor in restaurant management. Fully expecting to pursue a career in the food service industry Nancy took her first job as a food supervisor at the Colonnade Company in Philadelphia, PA. After several years there a new Hyatt hotel opened practically in her backyard in South Jersey. Wanting to rid herself of the commute by train to Philadelphia everyday; Nancy applied at the Hyatt Cherry Hill, NJ. Her first position as "low man on the totem pole" was as a restaurant hostess. While still in the hostess position she was chosen to help with a sales "blitz" in the sales and marketing department of the hotel. That was the beginning of her life long career in the sales industry.

Staying with Hyatt Hotels Corporation for 12 years in sales and marketing Nancy served as a sales manager at the Hyatt Regency Dallas, TX, Hyatt Regency Grand Cypress, Orlando, FL and finally as Director of Sales for the Hyatt Regency Princeton in New Jersey where she met her husband Jack. A year after they married she left the hotel business to raise their family. They have two sons; David and Steven. As a stay-at-home mom Nancy was always working in sales in some capacity and continues to do so with a fabulous company called Arbonne International. She is an independent consultant with this 29-yea-old Swiss health and wellness company. Arbonne affords her the opportunity of a flexible schedule to still be "around" for her sons, and healthy products to take care of the whole family. Arbonne also offers a generous compensation plan which helps her fulfill her lifelong dreams. Nancy continues to reside in New Jersey while raising her "Jersey Boys."

Nancy Munn
Phone: 609-462-1828
Website: http://www.headtotoebodycare.myarbonne.com

**Diana Nichols (Rule 23)** has over 30 years of small business and entrepreneurial success. Diana brings knowledge, grounded wisdom, enthusiasm, and a wealth of creative resources to everything she does. As a business and life coach, workshop creator and facilitator, artist, web/database developer and successful entrepreneur, Diana assists her clients in combining creativity and practicality into a unique experience of success.

Diana is passionate about creating beauty, simplicity, usefulness, and fun in all of her endeavors. Her latest project, Just Imagine That Coaching©, empowers entrepreneurs and small business people to incorporate imagination, creativity and innovation into all areas of their business. Combining their business experience, creativity, coaching skills, and sense of adventure, she and her partner Karen Stone have created a comprehensive program and a wealth of resources that give clients an edge in today's changing market.

Diana Nichols, LCC
Email: diana@diananichols.com
Website: http://JustImagineThatCoaching.com
　　　　http://LinkedIn.com/in/diananichols
　　　　http://Twitter.com/diananichols

**Tiffany Odutoye (Rule 41)** is the Founder and Chief Visionary Officer of Virtual Partner, LLC, a Virtual Assistance and Business Management Practice. She also recently launched a new brand, Talk Social Networking, LLC, to offer social media training and support. Consumed by a need to test out new Web 2.0 technology for her Virtual Assistance practice, Odutoye became a social media specialist quite by chance. The rapid development and real-time results of social media soon had her blogging about it. As ongoing business requests from clients emerged, Odutoye obtained her certification as a Social Media Specialist from VAClassroom and continued to learn from experts in the field. This self-sought training soon positioned her to strategize with businesses on their social media marketing plans.

The more she helped clients, the more Odutoye saw the need for group workshops. She envisioned the concept as a way of reaching larger numbers of people with the same questions. And the idea of a full-day, hands-on workshops was born to complement her VA practice. The Assistant Organizer for the Columbus Social Media Networking (Tweetup) Group, Odutoye is also the author of a forthcoming book on Social Media called 'Now What Do I Do? An entrepreneur's guide to getting to next with Social Media,' slated for a June 2009 release. A *summa cum laude* graduate of St. Petersburg State University, Odutoye is a resident of Granville, Ohio, where she enjoys community educational work, reading, traveling, cultural dance, and classical music. She describes herself as driven, a visionary, optimistic and a lifelong learner. Above all, she cherishes opportunities for spiritual and family connections.

Tiffany Odutoye (oh-do-toy)
Phone: 740- 877-1320
Email: info@virtualpartner.biz
Websites: http://www.talksocialnetworking.com
            http://www.virtualpartner.biz
Twitter: http://twitter.com/virtualpartner
Facebook: http://www.profile.to/virtualpartner/
Linkedin: http://www.linkedin.com/in/virtualpartner

**Sheila Pearl (Rule 27)** is a co-author in 'WAKE UP WOMEN: Be Happy, Healthy and Wealthy,' a guidebook filled with golden nuggets of wisdom by 50 coaches from around the world. She is also a keynote speaker, seminar leader and life coach. Sheila has been a family therapist and spiritual leader in the New York/New Jersey metropolitan area for over 25 years. She is author of her first book in a series of "Pearls of Wisdom"—'STILL LIFE: A Spiritual Guidebook for Family Caregivers.' She is also co-author with Laura Moritz of 'The Winning Connection—the Networker's Guide to Wealth-Building Synergistic Relationships.'

Sheila Pearl
Email: Info@LifeCoachSheila.com
Website: http://www.SheilaPearl.com

**Meghan Peters (Rule 38)** owns her own business as a sales representative with Wildtree, an all-natural food company. Meghan became a licensee with The Joy of Connecting® in December 2008 to meet other businesswomen in the community and to help professional women prosper. The message of the article comes from personal trial and error; from a girl who loved to talk on the phone to a woman who only wanted to type, she had to re-educate herself to personally make that connection! Meghan presently currently lives in Wauwatosa, WI; a suburb of Milwaukee. She would like to thank all of the people that have supported her unconditionally: Bean, family and friends, Wildtree and the JOC sisters.

Meghan Peters
Email: Mjp3211@aol.com
Website: http://www.meghanpeters.mywildtree.com

**Valerie Pierce (Rule 5)** was told that as a baby she didn't have a first word; she had a first paragraph! During her school years, she was a cheerleader, President of her senior class, chaplain of the student body and very active with her church youth group. While in high school she developed a skill for cold calling. Valerie did cold calling for a non-profit group directly linked with the Fellowship for Christian Athletes. Previously, she worked in a high-end salon and spa where she "cut her teeth" in the rule of persistence. While there, Valerie read numerous books on guerilla marketing sales and telemarketing. Those skills were carried over to being a successful Independent Beauty Consultant with Mary Kay Cosmetics. In 2007 Valerie earned the esteemed position of Queen of Sales for her Unit. As we all know, getting customers is good and keeping customers is better.

Recently, Valerie has been involved in several networking groups including The Cobb County Chamber of Commerce, The Powder Springs Business Association and The Kennesaw Business Association. Valerie is also a licensee for The Joy of Connecting® (http://www.thejoyofconnecting.com) in Kennesaw, Georgia. Valerie loves to meet people and engage in conversations. This trait helped her launch a successful grass roots marketing company in October 2008.

Valerie Pierce
Independent Mary Kay Consultant
Grass roots marketing expert
Phone: 770-367-1390
Email: jvpierce@att.net
Website: http://www.marykay.com/vpierce1

**C. Denese Sampson (Rule 8)** is a native Atlantan and the oldest daughter of five children. In November 2008, she became an independent sales representative for Silpada Designs, a fine sterling silver jewelry company based out of Kansas. Silpada has opened many doors for Denese to make connections through social networking and marketing as she continues to strive toward building a team in Georgia. She enjoys the one-on-one connections made at jewelry showcases in her clients' homes and businesses. Most recently, Denese also became affiliated with Simply Fun, a direct marketing company of family friendly games and products that bring people together through play. Denese's family lifestyle fits right into the mission of Simply Fun, and she looks forward to opening even more opportunities in this capacity. In her "regular" job, Denese has been employed with the State Senate as a Legislative Assistant since 1996, serving over ten state Senators and under three Governors.

Denese's best work is seen in her five wonderful children! Her oldest son and his wife have a toddler, her oldest daughter is a college sophomore, and three younger children are school aged. Together, they are the best example of what a Simply Fun family game night feels like!

Denese is driven by a deep passion and commitment to serving her community. She is very active in the children's schools and is a volunteer soccer coach. Denese believes in being an excellent servant in all her endeavors.

C. Denese Sampson, Morrow JOC Licensee
Phone: 404.272.3761
Email: denese.sampson@gmail.com
Websites: http://www.thejoyofconnecting.com
http://www.mysilpada.com/denese.sampson
http://www.denesesampson.simplyfun.com

**Karen Stone, MSW, LCC, CCIM (Rule 17)** has been motivating, mentoring and educating people for over 30 years. As a Life, Career and Business Coach, a writer, a speaker, and a seminar creator and leader, Karen uses her practical wisdom, boundless energy and enthusiasm to inspire and guide others as they live their lives fully, uncover their magnificence and live on purpose with passion. Drawing on her extensive range of corporate, entrepreneurial and personal growth expertise, Karen offers her clients a unique synthesis of grounded 'how-to' information, optimism, and an unwavering belief in each person's ability to achieve their definition of success.

Karen specializes in coaching individuals and groups through transitions with a focus on finding opportunities and expanding possibilities in times of change. Her passion is being an empowering, useful resource to others.

With partner Diana Nichols, Karen has launched Just Imagine That Coaching©, a comprehensive, experiential program for entrepreneurs and small business people who are ready to take their businesses to the next level of success. By combining their creativity, business experience and coaching skills, Karen and Diana have created a valuable resource that empowers businesspeople to incorporate imagination, creativity and innovation into all areas of their business, giving them an edge in today's changing marketplace. Karen believes that life is an unfolding adventure that is just waiting for us to say "Yes!" She lives happily, creatively and gratefully in Atlanta with her life partner, Rich, and their animal family.

Karen Stone
Emails: k.stone@mindspring.com
          Karen@KarenStoneCoach.com
Websites: http://www.JustImagineThatCoaching.com
          http://www.KarenStoneCoach.com

**Jolynn Van Asten's (Rule 35)** life work is to support men and women who desire to succeed in owning their own business, as well as assisting professionals who desire to grow the amount of warm referrals they receive daily. Whether a business is brick and mortar or home based, certain skills with verbiage will drive it to the top. Jolynn's carefully crafted verbiage coaching is sought after by professionals who desire to succeed in business as well as to communicate better with friends and loved ones. From corporate clients, to stay-at-home moms, she carefully assesses the needs and desires of an individual to assist them in building a future that is satisfying. She knows first hand the distresses and pleasures of balancing home, family, relationships a career and more.

Jolynn is a certified Mindful Life Coach, a leader in her direct sales organization: http://www.SendBetterCards.com, a freelance writer, published author, and Joy of Connecting licensee. Currently Jolynn is finishing her degree in Psychology as well. She lives in the historic town of Kohler, WI, with her husband Terry and five of their 6 children. Watch for informational books by Jolynn to be released in 2009. She may be contacted via email for verbiage coaching or other consulting. She is available for a free ½ hour consultation. Call today to set up a time to learn more about growing your business. Mention that you discovered her in the 42 Rules book, for an extra gift when you call.

Jolynn Van Asten
Phone: 920-917-7272
Email: calljolynn@sendbettercards.com

**Annette Walden (Rule 14)** is a multi-talented and multi-skilled individual with a background in sales, customer service, management, and marketing. During her years with a leading computer company, she earned the title of "Master Facilitator" in the "Investment in Excellence" program, which communicates the importance of personal growth through goal setting.

After spending almost 20 years in the corporate world, Annette now has her own business, Painted Lady Enterprises. She enjoys her role as Marketing Solutions Consultant specializing in helping businesses build relationships with prospects and existing clients for a source of endless referrals by providing gifts, greeting cards, imprinted ad specialty promotional products and other business resources. Her passion is helping other entrepreneurs grow in their personal development as well as helping them grow their business. She provides marketing consultations and also speaks to groups on a variety of topics. She is currently a member and ambassador of her local Chamber of Commerce, a member of Business Networking International, the American Business Women's Association, and licensee for The Joy of Connecting®.

Annette Walden
Email: Annette@PaintedLadyEnterprises.com
Website: http://www.PaintedLadyEnterprises.com

**Phyllis Wallace (Rule 18)** has over 16 years of hands-on experience in human resources for global Fortune 500 Companies. Phyllis most recently began a new career in direct sales. In 2008, Blessings Unlimited ranked her first among its top performers in sales and named her a Founding Leader for its Circle of Honor. Her community activities include career coaching and mentoring and she is frequently called upon to help others in their personal and professional lives. She resides in a suburb outside of Atlanta.

Phyllis Wallace
Independent Consultant and Founding Leader, Blessings Unlimited
Phone: H: 770-434-0794 | C: 678-360-4112
Email: pdw1@charter.net
Website: http://www.misspdw.blessingsdirect.com

**Vicki Wallace (Rule 11)** has 23+ years experience working in corporate America. She is a very self-motivated, people-oriented professional with strong marketing and communications as well as corporate training. Vicki has a passion for personal and professional development and has spent 12 years in corporate training. She is a consummate leader with strong organizational skills and is currently partnered with world renowned speaker/trainer Brian Tracy. Vicki is excited to help you invest in yourself by masterminding with top experts and assisting you in reaching your business objectives.

Vicki was a Founding Member for eWomenNetwork as well as their first National Executive Director. She is also a licensed realtor with Coldwell Banker Realtors helping buyers find their dream home. She graduated *magna cum laude* from College of Mount St. Joseph in Cincinnati, Ohio with a dual degree in management and marketing. Vicki has recognized with the following awards:

- International Who's Who of Professional and Business Women
- Who's Who in Women Executives
- Who's Who in Midwest Executives
- American Marketing Association
- Direct Marketing Association
- National Speakers Association
- American Society for Training and Development
- Academic Merit Award, College of Mount St. Joseph
- Ohio House of Representatives Honor Award, College of Mount St. Joseph
- Junior Achievement

Grow, Be Inspired and Go After Your Dreams!

Vicki Wallace
Dayton/Cincinnati/Springboro, OH
Phone: 937-545-0944
Email: Vicki.Wallace@earthlink.net
Website: http://www.ilearningglobal.biz/globalexperts

**Cassandra Wind (Rule 37)** is a mother of three and runs a full-time alternative medicine practice, Wind Touch Healing, LLC. Her practice in alternative therapies has evolved over 15 years. Wind Touch Healing provides acupuncture, craniosacral therapy and nutritional counseling to address issues of stress, headaches, acid reflux, IBS, low libido, depression, menstrual irregularities, pain, fibromyalgia, tendonitis and more. She promotes health to keep you doing the things you enjoy and believes life is best lived fully. She holds a Master of Science in Oriental Medicine and over 25 years of experience in western diagnostic medicine. She interned as a student at the University of Traditional Chinese Medicine in Guangzhou, China, and holds licenses in the State of Wisconsin for Acupuncture and Massage Therapy.

Cassandra's mission is to help educate individuals on how to utilize and when to integrate eastern and western healing therapies. Her passion of exploring healing in ancient cultures and utilizing this wisdom in her integrative medicine practice creates a more expansive approach to healing. As Cassandra states, "Together, these practices can help individuals attain optimal health."

Cassandra Wind - Founder/CEO
Email: windtouchhealing@sbcglobal.net
Website: http://www.windtouchhealing.com

**Linda Wind (Rule 40)** is President of Wind Enterprises® Inc., a corporation committed to the personal and professional development of women. With an MBA from the University of Dallas in Irving, Texas, and a BBA from Texas A&M University at Corpus Christi, she was a recipient of the Y Women in Careers Award, a Mentor for the Georgia 100 Mentor Exchange Program, was the recipient of NAWBO's 2005 Inspiration of the Year Award, and selected by 'Women Looking Ahead Magazine' as one of the 100 most powerful and influential women in Georgia. Linda has recently been named to the inaugural list of The International Alliance for Women "TIAW World of Difference 100." As one of 50 exceptional women from 15 countries, Wind was honored for her contributions to education and leadership development leading to the economic empowerment of women. Her 20-year corporate career has included positions with IBM, Savin, Sharp Electronics Corporation, Pitney Bowes, Panasonic and AirTouch.

Linda is a past-president of the Atlanta Women's Network, was on the founding board of the Atlanta Women's Alliance, is on the advisory board for ProWIN and is actively involved with the Georgia Commission on Women. She is the Founding Chair of the Possible Woman Foundation International, a 501C3 that awards academic scholarships to older women in need returning to school. She has also served on the Boards of Directors for the YWCA, American Heart Association, Northside Hospital, Sales and Marketing Executives, NAWBO, Norcross Rotary and Board of Directors Network. She is a graduate of Leadership Corpus Christi, Leadership Atlanta (1999), and Leadership America (2003). She is also a member of the International Women's Forum. Her Possible Woman® leadership conferences, weekend retreats for women and Wind Enterprises™ (WE) Membership Program have been featured in several local and national publications including the 'Wall Street Journal.'

Linda Wind
Email: Linda@WindEnterprises.com
Website: http://www.windenterprises.com

# About the Authors

**Bonnie Ross-Parker (Rule 2)** a.k.a. "America's Connection Diva," is a multi-dimensional businesswomen and entrepreneur with a background in education, franchise development, publishing, mentorship, network marketing, and community development. She combines vision with a unique set of skills. Formerly the Associate Publisher of 'The Gazette Newspaper/Atlanta,' she focuses her energies on supporting women. Bonnie is a graduate of George Washington University, and earned a Certification in Network Marketing at the University of Illinois. Several of her articles on owning one's own business and entrepreneurship have appeared in publications including 'Wealth Building,' 'Home Business Magazine,' 'Business to Business' and 'Entrepreneur's Business Start-Ups.' In 2002, Bonnie received The Athena Award an honor designed to acknowledge women of leadership in cities throughout the United States. In September 2005 she was honored by the Women's Leadership Exchange, a New York based organization, as an Influential Woman of Georgia and currently serves on their Atlanta Advisory Board. Bonnie is a featured speaker with the Direct Selling Women's Alliance.

Bonnie was honored by The International Toastmaster's Organization of Georgia with their annual Communication and Leadership Award in May 2006. She's the author of 'Walk In My Boots—The Joy of Connecting,' and 'Y.O.U. Set A High Standard for Being Human.' Passionate about enriching the lives of businesswomen, in August 2002, Bonnie licensed an innovative customer acquisition/marketing program for women called The Joy of Connecting® (JOC). Over two thousand women have experienced JOC in her home since the launch. Currently, there are locations nationwide for professional women, entrepreneurs and business owners to share resources, establish and strengthen relationships and to grow their businesses by networking with one another. The Joy of Connecting® is looking to expand in additional cities throughout the country.

Bonnie Ross-Parker
Phone: 770-333-7923
Email: bootgirl@TheJOYofConnecting.com
Website: http://www.TheJOYofConnecting.com

**Cindy Elsberry (Rule 9)** is CEO and Founder of Bumble Bee Virtual Assistant Services. She began her career as an administrative assistant after high school. While working full time she earned her Bachelor's in Business Administration. After over twenty years in the corporate world, Cindy was thrown into the world of the unemployed.

Seeking a way to utilize her various skills, she established Bumble Bee Virtual Assistant Services in 2008. Cindy is able to handle any type administrative work you would have an in-office assistant perform—well, except for making coffee! Some of her services and abilities include: Creation and email blasts of newsletters, creating/maintaining databases, manuscript editing, proofreading of marketing materials, bookkeeping, QuickBooks and other software training, payroll, Internet research and much more.

Cindy Elsberry
Email: CindyElsberry@gmail.com
Website: http://www.bumblebeevirtualassistantservices.com

# Write Your Own Rules

You can write your own 42 Rules book, and we can help you do it—from initial concept, to writing and editing, to publishing and marketing. If you have a great idea for a 42 Rules book, then we want to hear from you.

As you know, the books in the 42 Rules series are practical guidebooks that focus on a single topic. The books are written in an easy-to-read format that condenses the fundamental elements of the topic into 42 Rules. They use realistic examples to make their point and are fun to read.

### Two Kinds of 42 Rules Books

42 Rules books are published in two formats: the single-author book and the contributed-author book. The single-author book is a traditional book written by one author. The contributed-author book (like '42 Rules for Working Moms') is a compilation of Rules, each written by a different contributor, which support the main topic. If you want to be the sole author of a book or one of its contributors, we can help you succeed!

### 42 Rules Program

A lot of people would like to write a book, but only a few actually do. Finding a publisher, and distributing and marketing the book are challenges that prevent even the most ambitious of authors to ever get started.

At 42 Rules, we help you focus on and be successful in the writing of your book. Our program concentrates on the following tasks so you don't have to.

- **Publishing:** You receive expert advice and guidance from the Executive Editor, copy editors, technical editors, and cover and layout designers to help you create your book.

- **Distribution:** We distribute your book through the major book distribution channels, like Baker and Taylor and Ingram, Amazon.com, Barnes and Noble, Borders Books, etc.

- **Marketing:** 42 Rules has a full-service marketing program that includes a customized Web page for you and your book, email registrations and campaigns, blogs, webcasts, media kits and more.

Whether you are writing a single-authored book or a contributed-author book, you will receive editorial support from 42 Rules Executive Editor, Laura Lowell, author of '42 Rules of Marketing,' which was rated Top 5 in Business Humor and Top 25 in Business Marketing on Amazon.com (December 2007), and author and Executive Editor of '42 Rules for Working Moms.'

## Accepting Submissions

If you want to be a successful author, we'll provide you the tools to help make it happen. Start today by answering the following questions and visit our website at http://superstarpress.com/ for more information on submitting your 42 Rules book idea.

Super Star Press is now accepting submissions for books in the 42 Rules book series. For more information, email info@superstarpress.com or call 408-257-3000.

## Other Happy About Books

### 42 Rules™ for Working Moms

This book assembles the guidance of contributors who offer their thoughts on topics ranging from raising polite children and making time for yourself, as well as your mate, to losing the mommy guilt and delegating at home.

Paperback:$19.95
eBook:$14.95

### 42 Rules™ for 24-Hour Success on LinkedIn

This is a user-friendly guidebook designed to help you leverage the power of LinkedIn to build visibility, make connections and support your brand.

Paperback:$19.95
eBook:$14.95

## Rule #1: Stop Talking!

**RULE #1: STOP TALKING!**

A Guide to Listening

by
Linda Eve Diamond

Learn to become a savvy, critical listener and listen to yourself to create the life you truly want.

Paperback:$16.95
eBook:$14.95

---

## The Successful Introvert

**S**UCCESSFUL
**INTROVERT**

How to...
ENHANCE YOUR
**JOB SEARCH**
AND ADVANCE
YOUR CAREER

WENDY GELBERG

HappyAbout info

This book is intended to both enlighten and empower readers with specific strategies to use in everyday personal and professional activities so that they can achieve greater success in their lives.

Paperback:$19.95
eBook:$14.95

---

Purchase these books at Happy About
http://happyabout.info/
or at other online and physical bookstores.

## A Message From Super Star Press™

Thank you for your purchase of this 42 Rules Series book. It is available online at: http://happyabout.info/42rules/effectiveconnections.php or at other online and physical bookstores. To learn more about contributing to books in the 42 Rules series, check out http://superstarpress.com.

Please contact us for quantity discounts at sales@superstarpress.com

If you want to be informed by email of upcoming books, please email bookupdate@superstarpress.com.